v010216
pc: 254
ISBN: 1932733906

Adobe Captivate 9: Beyond the Essentials

"Skills and Drills" Learning

Kevin Siegel

"Skills and Drills" Learning

Contents

Branching 49
   Use Buttons to Create a Branch 49
      Branching Confidence Check...50
   Explore the Branching View...51
Groups...54
   Create a Slide Group...54
Aggregating 56
   Publish SWFs 56
      Publishing Confidence Check 57
   Aggregate SWFs..58
      Aggregator Confidence Check...59

Module 4: Random Quizzes
GIFT Files 62
   Review a GIFT File..62
   Import a GIFT File into a Project 63
Question Pools..64
   Create Question Pools 64
      Question Pools Confidence Check 65
   Move Questions to Pools 66
      Moving Questions to Pools Confidence Check 67
Random Question Slides 68
   Insert Random Question Slides 68
      Random Questions Confidence Check 69

Module 5: Accessible eLearning
Accessibility and Captivate 72
   Set Document Information..73
   Enable Accessibility..74
Accessibility Text 75
   Add Accessibility Text to Slides...75
   Import Slide Audio..77
      Accessibility Text Confidence Check......................................78
Shortcut Keys...80
   Add Shortcut Keys 80
      Keyboard Shortcut Confidence Check.....................................82
Closed Captioning 83
   Add Closed Captions 83
      Closed Captions Confidence Check 86
Tab Order...89
   Set a Tab Order..89
      Tab Order Confidence Check...91

Module 6: Variables and Widgets
Variables 94
   Add Project Information..94
   Insert a System Variable 95
      Variable Preview Confidence Check 96
   Edit a System Variable 97
      System Variables Confidence Check 98
User Variables 99
   Create a User Variable...99
   Use a Variable to Gather Learner Data 101
      User-Defined Variables Confidence Check.............................. 103
Widgets.. 104
   Insert and Format a Widget 104

Notes

iCONLOGiC
"Skills and Drills" Learning

About This Book

This Section Contains Information About:

The Author

Kevin Siegel is the founder and president of IconLogic, Inc. He has written hundreds of step-by-step computer training books on applications such as *Adobe Captivate, Articulate Storyline, Adobe RoboHelp, Adobe Presenter, Adobe Technical Communication Suite, Adobe Dreamweaver, Adobe InDesign, Microsoft Word, Microsoft PowerPoint, QuarkXPress,* and *TechSmith Camtasia Studio.*

Kevin spent five years in the U.S. Coast Guard as an award-winning photojournalist and has nearly three decades of experience as a print publisher, technical writer, instructional designer, and eLearning developer. He is a certified technical trainer, a veteran classroom instructor, and a frequent speaker at trade shows and conventions.

Kevin holds multiple certifications from companies such as Adobe and CompTIA. You can reach Kevin at **ksiegel@iconlogic.com**.

What This Book Teaches

This book is a continuation to my *Adobe Captivate 9: The Essentials* book, published in October 2015. In that book, my goal was to get you up and running using Captivate as quickly as possible. After completing *Adobe Captivate 9: The Essentials*, readers have a fair grasp of how to both record and produce eLearning lessons using Adobe Captivate. Key concepts in that book include, but are not limited to, adding standard objects such as captions, click boxes, text entry boxes, rollover captions, and images. Readers also learn how to record, edit, and insert audio into a Captivate project. And there are lessons on adding quizzes and publishing content as an SWF, HTML5, and PDF.

In this book, you are going to learn how to work with Video Demos (page 17), create a branching scenario (page 37), add Question Pools (page 61), and create eLearning content that is accessible to learners with disabilities (page 71). You will add user variables (page 93) and learner interactions (page 108) to a project that engages the learner at a personal level. You'll also learn about Actions (page 129) and how to create project templates (page 163). Then you will create responsive eLearning—content that reflows to fit multiple display sizes (page 185), perfect for mobile learners and desktop learners alike. And you'll learn how to set up and publish a project that reports scores to a Learning Management System (page 220).

Book Conventions

I believe that learners learn by doing. With that simple concept in mind, IconLogic books are created by trainers/authors with years of experience training adult learners. Before IconLogic books, our instructors rarely found a book that was perfect for a classroom setting. If the book was beautiful, odds were that the text was too small to read and hard to follow. If the text in a book was the right size, the quality of the exercises left something to be desired.

Finally tiring of using inadequate materials, our instructors started teaching without any books at all. Years ago we had many students ask if the in-class instruction came from a book. If so, they said they'd buy the book. That sparked an idea. We asked students—just like you—what they wanted in a workbook. You responded, and that methodology is used in this book and every IconLogic training manual.

This book has been divided into several modules. Because each module builds on lessons learned in a previous module, I recommend that you complete each module in succession. Each module guides you through lessons step-by-step. Here is the lesson key:

❑ instructions for you to follow look like this

If you are expected to type anything or if something is important, it is set in bold type like this:

❑ type **9** into the text field

When you are asked to press a key on your keyboard, the instruction looks like this:

❑ press [**shift**]

I hope you enjoy the book. If you have any comments or questions, please see page xiii for our contact information.

Confidence Checks

As you move through the lessons in this book, you will come across the little guy at the right. He indicates a Confidence Check. Throughout each module, you are guided through hands-on, step-by-step exercises. But at some point you'll have to fend for yourself. That is where Confidence Checks come in. Please be sure to complete each of the challenges because some exercises build on completed Confidence Checks.

Book Requirements

This workbook teaches you how to use Adobe Captivate version 9. The Adobe Captivate software does not come with this book. The software can be downloaded directly from Adobe (**www.adobe.com/products/captivate.html**). You do not need to purchase Captivate to learn Captivate; the free trial version of the software can be downloaded via the link above. The only limitation on the trial is that it lasts for 30 days from the day you first run the software on your computer.

You need speakers (or a headset) to complete the activities about Accessible eLearning. During that module (page 71), you import audio files and learn how to create closed captions.

Data Files (Captivate Project Assets)

To complete the lessons in this book, you need the Adobe Captivate 9 software (you can download a free trial from the Adobe website). You also need assets to play with as you learn Captivate (such as Captivate 9 project files, images, and audio files). Fortunately, you don't have to create those assets... I've created them for you and you can download them from the Iconlogic website for free.

Windows users: Work through the activity below; **Mac users:** Skip the activity below and move on to page xi.

Student Activity: Download the Windows Data Files

1. Download the student data files necessary to complete the lessons presented in this book.

   ❑ start a web browser and visit the following web address:
   http://www.iconlogic.com/pc
   ❑ click the **Captivate 9: Beyond The Essentials** link

2. Save the file to your computer. After the file downloads, close the web browser.

3. Extract the data files.

   ❑ find the **Captivate9BeyondData** file you just downloaded to your computer
   ❑ double-click the file to execute it (even though the file is an EXE file, it's not a program; rather it's an archive containing zipped data files)
   ❑ if presented with a Security Warning dialog box, click **Run** or **Yes**

   The WinZip Self-Extractor opens.

   ❑ confirm **C:** appears in the **Unzip to folder** area (only change the **Unzip to folder** if you are prohibited from installing assets directly to your C drive)

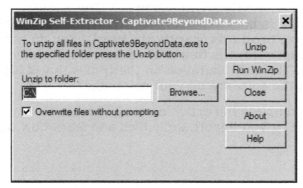

   ❑ click the **Unzip** button

   You will be notified that several files were unzipped.

   ❑ click the **OK** button and then click the **Close** button

   A **Captivate9BeyondData** folder has been installed on your computer. As you move through the lessons in this book, you will be working with the files within this folder. You can skip the next activity and turn to page xii.

Student Activity: Download the Mac Data Files

1. Download the student data files necessary to complete the lessons presented in this book.

   ☐ start your web browser and go to the following web address:
   http://www.iconlogic.com/mac

   ☐ click the **Captivate 9: Beyond The Essentials** link

   The zipped data files are typically downloaded to the **Downloads** folder on your Mac and automatically extracted into a folder named **Captivate9BeyondData**.

2. Move the data files folder to your desktop.

   ☐ find the **Captivate9BeyondData** folder and drag it to your desktop

Captivate's Preferences

Adobe Captivate is awesome. But like most computer programs, it can behave poorly. I've found that when Captivate gets sluggish on my computer or crashes, it's because I've got too many applications running and not enough resources. In that instance, closing all nonessential applications solves the problem.

However, there are times when nothing I do seems to help improve Captivate's performance (not even a system reboot). In those rare instances, I've found that resetting all of Captivate's Preferences cures what ails Captivate.

If you need to reset Captivate's Preferences, you'll appreciate an obscure utility that ships with Captivate that will reset all of the Preferences for you. Prior to beginning the first module in this book, I'd encourage you to reset your Captivate preferences so that your Captivate settings match those shown in the book.

Student Activity: Reset Captivate's Preferences

1. Ensure that Adobe Captivate isn't running.

2. Reset Captivate's Preferences.

   ❑ navigate to the folder where Captivate is installed on your computer

   Note: On Windows, the default location is typically **C:\Program Files\Adobe\Adobe Captivate 9**. On a Macintosh, the default location is typically **Applications > Adobe Captivate 9**.

   ❑ open the **utils** folder

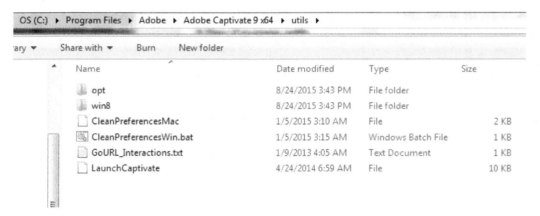

You'll find two files of particular interest within the **utils** folder: **CleanPreferencesMac** and **CleanPreferencesWin.bat**.

   ❑ double-click the file appropriate for your operating system

All of Captivate's application Preferences will be reset to the way they were the first day Captivate was installed on your computer.

How Software Updates Affect This Book

This book was written specifically to teach you how to use **Adobe Captivate version 9.0**. At the time this book was written, Captivate 9 was the latest and greatest version of the Captivate software available from Adobe.

With each major release of Captivate, my intention is to write a new book to support that version and make it available within 30-60 days of the software being released by Adobe. From time to time, Adobe announces service releases/patches for Captivate that fix bugs or add functionality. For instance, I would expect Adobe to update Captivate with a patch or two within a few months of the release of Captivate 9. That patched version might be called Captivate **9.01** or **9.1**. Usually these updates are minor (bug fixes) and have little or no impact on the lessons presented in this book. However, Adobe sometimes makes significant changes to the way Captivate looks or behaves, even with minor patches. (Such was the case when Adobe updated Captivate from version 5 to 5.5—about a dozen features were added, and a few panels were actually renamed, throwing readers of my books into a tizzy.)

Because it is not possible for me to recall and update printed books, some instructions you are asked to follow in this book may not match the patched/updated version of Captivate that you might be using. If something on your screen does not match what I am showing in the book, please visit the Adobe Captivate 9 product page on my website for possible updates (http://www.iconlogic.com/adobe-captivate-9-beyond-essentials-workbook.html).

Special Thanks

No book is perfect... not even this one. Nevertheless, every attempt was made to minimize errors (grammatically, editorially, and in the step-by-step instructions). I'd like to thank Ellie Abrams for her proofreading. The following people either contributed directly to this book's content or served as a volunteer beta tester (the beta testers did a remarkable job ensuring the accuracy of this book's activities): Alison Leese, Barbara Ash, Lori Smith, Jennie Ruby, AJ Walther, Michael Mizen, Bob Cunningham, and Cheryl Bosarge.

Contacting IconLogic

IconLogic, Inc.
1582 Indian Bluffs Dr., Maineville, OH, 45039 | 410.956.4949
Web: **www.iconlogic.com** | Email: **info@iconlogic.com**

Notes

iCONLOGiC

"Skills and Drills" Learning

Rank Your Skills

Before starting this book, complete the skills assessment on the next page.

Skills Assessment

How This Assessment Works

Below you will find 10 course objectives for *Adobe Captivate 9: Beyond The Essentials*. **Before starting the book:** Review each objective and rank your skills using the scale next to each objective. A rank of ① means **No Confidence** in the skill. A rank of ⑤ means **Total Confidence**. After you've completed this assessment, go through the entire book. **After finishing the book:** Review each objective and rank your skills now that you've completed the book. Most people see dramatic improvements in the second assessment after completing the lessons in this book.

Before-Class Skills Assessment

1. I can edit a Text Capture Template.   ①   ②   ③   ④   ⑤
2. I can create a Slide Group.   ①   ②   ③   ④   ⑤
3. I can aggregate published SWFs.   ①   ②   ③   ④   ⑤
4. I can create Question Pools.   ①   ②   ③   ④   ⑤
5. I can add Accessibility Text to slides.   ①   ②   ③   ④   ⑤
6. I can create a Responsive Project.   ①   ②   ③   ④   ⑤
7. I can create a User Variable.   ①   ②   ③   ④   ⑤
8. I can create a Master Slide.   ①   ②   ③   ④   ⑤
9. I can create a Conditional Action.   ①   ②   ③   ④   ⑤
10. I can create a Manifest File.   ①   ②   ③   ④   ⑤

After-Class Skills Assessment

1. I can edit a Text Capture Template.   ①   ②   ③   ④   ⑤
2. I can create a Slide Group.   ①   ②   ③   ④   ⑤
3. I can aggregate published SWFs.   ①   ②   ③   ④   ⑤
4. I can create Question Pools.   ①   ②   ③   ④   ⑤
5. I can add Accessibility Text to slides.   ①   ②   ③   ④   ⑤
6. I can create a Responsive Project.   ①   ②   ③   ④   ⑤
7. I can create a User Variable.   ①   ②   ③   ④   ⑤
8. I can create a Master Slide.   ①   ②   ③   ④   ⑤
9. I can create a Conditional Action.   ①   ②   ③   ④   ⑤
10. I can create a Manifest File.   ①   ②   ③   ④   ⑤

IconLogic, Inc.
"Skills and Drills" Learning
Web: www.iconlogic.com | Email: info@iconlogic.com

iCONLOGiC
"Skills and Drills" Learning

Module 1: Caption Pre-Editing

In This Module You Will Learn About:

And You Will Learn To:

Rehearsals

You have been hired to create an eLearning course that teaches new employees at your company how to use **Notepad** (Windows) or **TextEdit** (Macintosh). One of the lessons you plan to record using Captivate includes how to change the page orientation within Notepad or TextEdit.

Here is a sample script showing the kind of detailed, step-by-step instructions you need to create or receive from a Subject Matter Expert (SME). You are expected to perform each step written below in either Notepad or TextEdit.

> Dear Captivate developer, using either Notepad or TextEdit, record the process of changing the Page Orientation from Portrait to Landscape and then back again (from Landscape to Portrait). Create the recording using a capture size of 800 x 600. Thanks. Your pal, the Subject Matter Expert.
>
> 1. Click the File menu.
>
> 2. Click the Page Setup menu item.
>
> 3. Click the Landscape orientation button.
>
> 4. Click the OK button.
>
> 5. Click the File menu.
>
> 6. Click the Page Setup menu item.
>
> 7. Click the Portrait orientation button.
>
> 8. Click the OK button.
>
> 9. Stop the recording process.

The script sounds simple. However, you will not know what kind of trouble you are going to get into unless you rehearse the script prior to recording the process with Captivate. Let's run a rehearsal, just as if you were a big-time movie director and you were in charge of a blockbuster movie.

Places everyone... and quiet on the set...

Student Activity: Rehearse a Script

1. Minimize (hide) Captivate.

2. Start either Notepad (Windows) or TextEdit (Mac).

   The process of starting either Notepad or TextEdit varies slightly, depending on your operating system. For instance, if you are using Windows, use the **Search** feature to start Notepad. If you are using a Mac, choose **Go > Applications**. Locate and open **TextEdit** and create a New document.

   In the images below, Notepad is pictured at the left; TextEdit is at the right.

   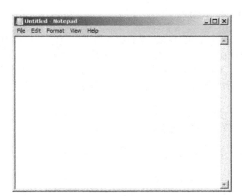 

3. Rehearse the script.

   ❏ using either Notepad or TextEdit (not Captivate), click the **File** menu

   ❏ click the **Page Setup** menu item

   ❏ from the **Orientation** area, click **Landscape**

   Note: In Notepad, Landscape is listed as the word "Landscape."
   In TextEdit, Landscape is the **second** tool (shown below).

   ❏ click the **OK** button

   ❏ click the **File** menu

   ❏ click the **Page Setup** menu item

   ❏ click the **Portrait** orientation button

   ❏ click the **OK** button

   The script worked perfectly and there were no surprises. You will perform these exact steps again in a few moments—for real. As you do, Captivate will record the steps by creating screen captures when you click the mouse.

   Note: If you are using Windows 8.1 or Windows 10 and the **File** menu opens outside the recording area, the menu will not be recorded. To resolve the issue, go to your computer's **Control Panel > Tablet PC Settings > Other** and enable **Left-handed**. Then try recording again.

Recording Custom Simulations

You can create software demonstrations or simulations using Captivate. Typical demonstrations include text captions that explain what's about to happen, and then a mouse automatically moves across the screen to perform the action. With a simulation, you can have text captions explaining a concept, just like a demonstration, but you can include interactive hotspots (click boxes) that let the user actually perform the required steps.

Between demonstrations and simulations, I recommend you create simulations, especially if you are working by yourself and don't have the resources to create both a demonstration and simulation for the same lesson. Why are simulations better? It's always better to let a user perform the step-by-step process you're trying to teach instead of allowing them to passively watch the steps.

When recording, I recommend you use Captivate's Custom recording mode. This mode effectively combines Captivate's Demonstration and Simulation modes. Using the Custom recording mode when you record, Captivate automatically adds text captions and click boxes throughout the lesson that engage your learner.

Student Activity: Set Recording Preferences

1. Leave Notepad or TextEdit running and start **Adobe Captivate**.

2. Set the Custom Mode Preferences for the simulation you are about to record.

   ❏ Windows users, choose **Edit > Preferences**;
   Mac users, choose **Adobe Captivate > Preferences**

   ❏ from the **Recording** category at the left of the dialog box, click **Modes**

   ❏ from the **Mode** drop-down menu, choose **Custom**

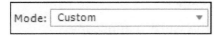

   ❏ from the **Captions** area, select **Add Text Captions**

   ❏ from the **Click Boxes** area, select **Add Click Boxes on Mouse Click**

   ❏ from the **Click Boxes** area, select **Failure Caption**

You selected **Add Text Captions** so that the Text Captions are added for you during the recording phase. *Nice.* And because the captions are written in the imperative, you may be able to use them in the new lesson with little editing. *Nicer.* Everything else has been left deselected except for **Click Boxes** and **Failure Caption** (like the simulation modes). These two settings result in a highly interactive simulation out of the box. *Nicest!*

3. Select a caption to use during the recording process.

   ❑ from the **Recording** category at the left of the dialog box, click **Defaults**

   ❑ from the **Text Caption** drop-down menu, ensure **[Default Capture Caption Style]** is selected

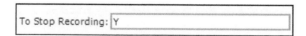

Global Preferences: Recording: Defaults

Objects:

Text Caption: [Default Capture Caption Style] ▾

The change you've just made won't be obvious until after you have recorded a software simulation. At that time, each of the text captions that get created in the simulation will use the Default Capture Caption Style. You'll soon use the Object Style Manager to control the look of the Default Capture Caption Style.

4. Customize the To Stop Recording keyboard shortcut.

   ❑ from the **Recording** category, select **Keys - (Global)**

   ❑ click in the **To Stop Recording** field and press the [**Y**] key on your keyboard

   The letter [**Y**] replaces the key that was in the field by default.

   To Stop Recording: Y

If you were to move forward and record a lesson using Captivate, you would press [**Y**] on your keyboard to end the recording process. You can customize the fields in this dialog box to suit your needs. For Windows users, the default key ([**End**]) works great.

5. Reset the default Recording Keys.

   ❑ still in the **Keys - (Global)** area, click the **Restore Defaults** button

   Restore Defaults

Mac users: On my Mac, the default **To Stop Recording** shortcut keys [**cmd**] [**enter**] only works on my MacBook Pro when I'm using an external extended keyboard. When I'm on the road, I change the keyboard shortcut to [**control**] [**e**] and things work perfectly every time. I would suggest that you experiment and find a keyboard shortcut that works best for you.

   ❑ click the **OK** button

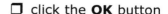

6. Use the Object Style Manager to format the Default Capture Caption Style.

   ❒ choose **Edit > Object Style Manager**

   The Object Style Manager dialog box opens.

   ❒ from the middle of the dialog box, select **[Default Capture Caption Style]**

   ❒ from the **Caption** drop-down menu, choose any **Caption Type** you like

   ❒ from the **Text Format** area, select any font (Family) and Size you like

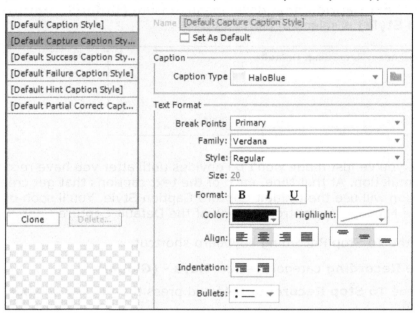

   ❒ click the **OK** button

Student Activity: Record a Simulation

1. Determine what Captivate records.

   ☐ on Captivate's Home screen, click the **New** button

   ☐ double-click **Software Simulation** (or choose **File > Record a New > Software Simulation**)

   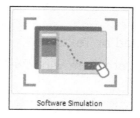

   The main Captivate interface hides, and the recording features open.

   On your computer display, notice two things besides Notepad or TextEdit. First, there is a large red box. This is Captivate's **Recording Area**. Second, there is a control panel containing Size and Recording Type areas. (Pictured below is a Windows desktop that shows Notepad with Captivate's recording window on top.)

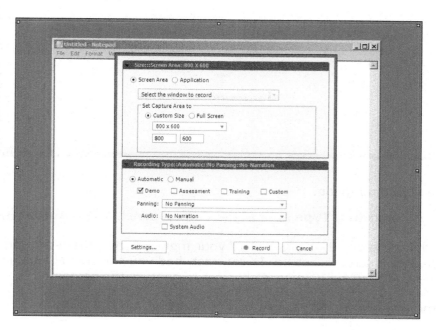

❑ from the top left of the control panel, select **Screen Area**

❑ from the **Set Capture Area to** area, select **Custom Size** and then choose **1024 x 627** from the drop-down menu

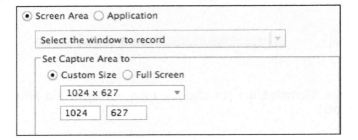

❑ drag the recording window so that it covers Notepad or TextEdit

❑ resize the Notepad or TextEdit window so that the program window fits nicely within the Recording Area

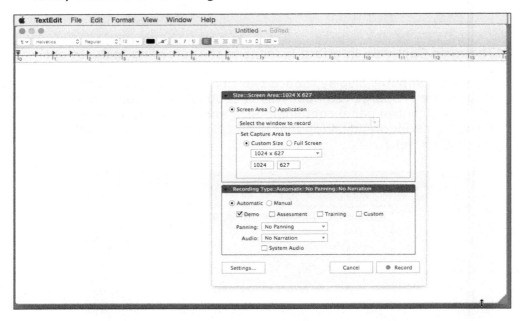

2. Select the recording mode.

❑ from the **Recording Type** area of the Control panel, select **Automatic**

With this option selected, every click of your mouse during the recording process creates a screen capture. In contrast, had you selected Manual mode, you would need to use a keyboard shortcut to capture the screen.

❑ from the **Recording Type** area, select **Custom**

❑ deselect the other modes as necessary

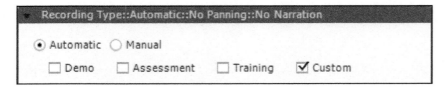

❑ ensure that **Panning** is set to **No Panning** and that **Audio** is set to **No Narration**

Panning:	No Panning ▾
Audio:	No Narration ▾
	☐ System Audio

Panning is appropriate when you want to record an action outside of the red Recording Area. It's not something you need to use in your upcoming recording. And because there's no voiceover audio needed for this lesson, you've left Audio set to No Narration. (Both Panning and Audio are covered in *"Adobe Captivate 9: The Essentials."*)

3. Record screen actions.

    ❑ click the **Record** button and, once the Countdown goes away, use your mouse to click the **File** menu within Notepad or TextEdit

    ❑ click the **Page Setup** menu item

    ❑ from the **Orientation** area, click **Landscape** and then click the **OK** button

    ❑ click the **File** menu

    ❑ click the **Page Setup** menu item

    ❑ click the **Portrait** orientation button and then click the **OK** button

4. Stop the recording process using the **Stop Recording** key (discussed on page 5).

    Note: If the recording doesn't end after pressing your Stop Recording keys, an alternative technique for stopping the recording process is to click the Captivate icon on the System Tray (Windows) or Dock (Mac).

5. Preview the project. (**Preview > Project**)

    As you move through the recording, there are Click Boxes (hot spots) that make this lesson 100 percent interactive. Also notice that the Text Captions are written in the imperative to encourage interactivity. There may be one or two captions you need to edit, and some of the background objects are likely misnamed, especially on the Mac side. Nevertheless, much of the work is done.

6. When finished previewing the lesson, close the preview.

7. Close the project (there is no need to save it).

Custom Recording Confidence Check

You have been asked to bookmark a website so it can be accessed quickly in the future. The process of creating a bookmark (Favorite) varies depending on the web browser you are using. For instance, if you are using **Internet Explorer**, you could choose the **Favorites** menu, click the **Add to Favorites** button and then click the **Add** button. If you are using **Google Chrome**, you could click the **Bookmark** button and then click the **Add** button. If you are using **Firefox**, you could choose **Bookmarks > Bookmark This Page**. If you are using **Safari**, show the Menu bar, choose **Bookmarks > Add Bookmark**, and then click the **Add** button.

Note: Browsers update frequently so if my instructions above are out of date, refer to your browser's Help system for instructions on bookmarking (or just Google it).

1. Using your browser of choice, use the **Custom** recording mode to create a simulation for creating a Bookmark (Favorite) for any website that you like.

   Not sure how to proceed or what exactly to record? Use Captivate to open the project named **Bookmarking.cptx** (you can find it within the Captivate9BeyondData folder). Preview the project and you'll see that I've created a simulation of the bookmarking process in each of the browsers mentioned above. You need to do the same in any browser you want. Forgotten how to record screen actions? See page 7.

2. When finished recording, save the new project to the **Captivate9BeyondData** folder as **CreateFavorite**.

3. Preview the project.

   Notice that there are text captions and interactivity, which is wonderful. However, none of the captions contain end-of-sentence punctuation. Although I am not a fan of end-of-sentence punctuation, many corporate style guides insist on end-of-sentence punctuation.

   Believe it or not, it is possible to "pre-edit" the text captions and change, among other things, the text that appears in the captions and the way Captivate treats end-of-sentence punctuation. You'll delve into that next. This little bit of wizardry just might save hours of content editing.

Caption Pre-Editing

When you record screen actions, Captivate can automatically create the text captions (provided you ensure **Add Text Captions** is selected via the Mode preferences). They are written in the imperative, which is fine. However, there are a couple of ways to write an instruction. For instance, if you want to instruct a learner to select the New command from a menu, you could lead the instruction with the word "Select" or "Choose." In effect, the text in the caption could be written two ways: "**Select** the New menu item" or "**Choose** the New menu item."

Captivate automatically uses the word "Select" when it creates text captions. If you want the text caption to use the word "Choose," you'd have to make the change manually after the recording process is complete. Although not difficult, this kind of editing is labor-intensive.

What about end-of-sentence punctuation? It's a hotly debatable topic. Do you or don't you? I don't, but you might.

To cut down on text editing in Captivate once the recording process is complete, you can pre-edit the text captions by modifying one of the language template files that are stored in the Captivate application folder on your hard drive. Captivate uses text capture template files to create the text captions.

Student Activity: Edit a Text Capture Template

1. Minimize/Hide Adobe Captivate.

2. Locate the file that controls the text that appears in automatic text captions.

   ☐ navigate to the folder where **Adobe Captivate 9** is installed on your computer (Windows users, the path is typically **Program Files/Adobe/ Adobe Captivate 9**; Mac users, Captivate is typically in a folder named **Adobe Captivate 9** in the **Applications** folder.)

   ☐ find (but do not open) **CaptureTextTemplates_English.rdl** file

   This next step is possibly the most important. You are going to create a copy of the English rdl file. If you mess up the duplicate rdl file, no worries because you can throw it away. The changes you are about to make to the duplicate rdl file will have no impact on the original rdl file.

3. Make a copy of the CaptureTextTemplates_English.rdl file.

   ☐ select the **CaptureTextTemplates_English.rdl** file and then **copy** and **paste** it into the Captivate 9 application folder (the current folder)

   Note: You may be prompted to confirm the action, which you should do. Because you are pasting a file directly within the application folder, you may be blocked completely because of limited read/write access to the application folder. In that case, you will need someone from your IT team to grant you read/write access to the Captivate application folder on your computer. Otherwise, you will be unable to complete the remaining steps in this module.

4. Rename the duplicate rdl file.

   ❏ change the name of the duplicate rdl file to
   CaptureTextTemplates_YourFirstName.rdl

   Check for typos in your new file name. In the image below, notice that Biff has created an rdl file named **CaptureTextTemplates_Biff.rdl**. You will be editing your personal rdl file next.

5. Open CaptureTextTemplates_YourFirstName.rdl with **NotePad** (Windows) or **TextEdit** (Mac).

   ❏ right-click your **rdl** file and choose **Open**

   If the file does not automatically open within NotePad (Windows) or TextEdit (Mac), you may need to lend a helping hand.

   ❏ Windows users, if a "Windows cannot open this file" dialog box (or similar) appears, choose **Select a program from a list of installed programs** and then click the OK button; Mac users, select **Choose Application**

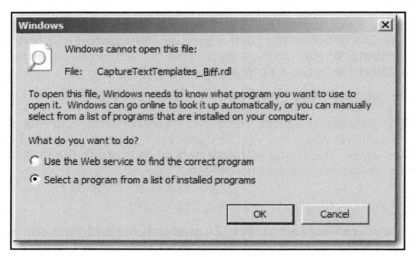

The **Open With** dialog box (Windows) or **Choose Application** dialog box (Mac) appears.

☐ Windows users, select **Notepad** from the list of available programs and click **OK**; Mac users, select **TextEdit**

In the images below, the Windows **Open With** dialog box is shown first; the Macintosh **Choose Application** dialog box is shown second.

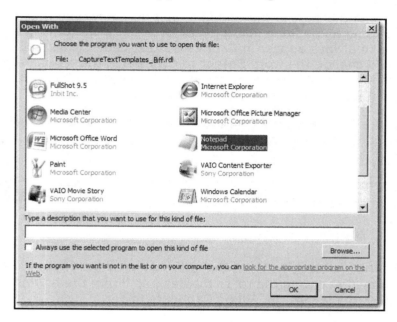

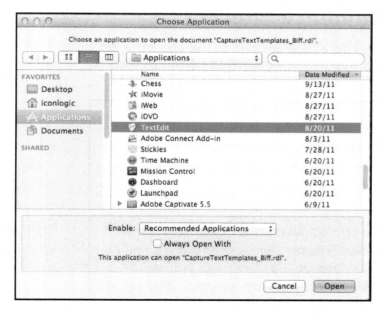

The rdl file opens in the text editor. If you are familiar with programming languages like HTML or XML, you will likely recognize the tags used in the document. If you do not have programming experience, no worries, you will be able to edit the template either way.

6. Edit the rdl file.

❏ scroll down to the part of the document shown below (if you have trouble finding the text, use the Find feature available in both Notepad and TextEdit to find **Object Name="Menu"**)

```
<Object Name="Menu" DefaultTemplate="Select the %s menu">
```

If you edit the text in this part of the template appropriately, you might be able to eliminate some text editing in Captivate later. For instance, if you want the word **Choose** to always appear in Captivate's text captions instead of the word **Select**, you'd change the word **Select** to **Choose** in the template prior to recording. And if you want the text captions to end with a period, all you'd need to do is add a period just to the left of the closing quote.

❏ at the end of the **Object Name="Menu"** line, click between the **u** in the word **menu** and the **closing quote**

❏ type a period (**.**)

```
<Object Name="Menu" DefaultTemplate="Select the %s menu.">
```

7. Save your work. (Keep the file open.)

Note: If you experience trouble saving the rdl file to your hard drive, you may succeed by first saving the rdl to the desktop. From there, you can copy/paste the rdl file into the Adobe Captivate folder.

RDL Editing Confidence Check

1. In the image below, I've added periods to the end of several lines of text. Spend a few moments adding periods on your own.

```
<Object Name="Menu" DefaultTemplate="Select the %s menu.">
  <Event Name="LeftDBClick" Template="Double-click the %s menu."/>
  <Event Name="RightClick" Template="Right Click the %s menu."/>
  <Event Name="RightDBClick" Template="Double-click the %s menu."/>
  <Event Name="MiddleDBClick" Template="Double-click the %s menu."/>
  <Event Name="KeyPress" Template="Press %s key for %s menu."/>
</Object>
<Object Name="MenuItem" DefaultTemplate="Select the %s menu item.">
  <Event Name="LeftDBClick" Template="Double-click the %s menu item."/>
  <Event Name="RightClick" Template="Right Click the %s menu item."/>
  <Event Name="RightDBClick" Template="Double-click the %s menu item."/>
  <Event Name="MiddleDBClick" Template="Double-click the %s menu item."/>
  <Event Name="KeyPress" Template="Press %s key for %s menu item."/>
```

2. As an experiment, change the words **Select the %s menu item** to **Choose the %s command.** (During the recording process, let's see if this has any effect on the text that appears in your text captions.)

3. Save and close the text file.

4. Return to Captivate and open Captivate's **Preferences** dialog box.

5. Select the **Recording** category from the list at the left.

6. Select your name from the **Generate Captions In** drop-down menu.

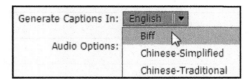

7. Using your browser of choice, use the **Custom** recording mode to create another simulation that covers the process of creating a Bookmark (Favorite) to any website you like. During the recording process, also select a menu or two and a menu item.

   Need help recording screen actions using Custom mode? See page 4.

8. When finished recording, save the new project to the **Captivate9BeyondData** folder as **CreateFavorite_CustomCaptions**.

9. Preview the project.

   The text captions should now contain end-of-sentence punctuation. In addition, if you used a menu when creating the Favorite, the text in the captions where you selected a menu command should now begin with **Choose** instead of **Select** and end with **command** instead of **menu item**.

   Notes: Changes made to an RDL file will have no effect on existing Captivate project. Only new recordings that use your RDL template will use your RDL settings. And you can elect to go back and use the original English rdl file at any time. Prior to recording new screen actions, display the **Preferences** dialog box, **Recording** category. Choose **English** from the **Generate Captions In** drop-down menu.

10. Close the preview.

11. Save and close all open projects.

Notes

_____

_____

_____

_____

_____

_____

_____

_____

_____

_____

_____

_____

_____

_____

_____

_____

_____

_____

_____

_____

_____

_____

_____

_____

_____

_____

_____

_____

_____

_____

_____

_____

_____

_____

iCONLOGiC

"Skills and Drills" Learning

Module 2: Video Demos

In This Module You Will Learn About:

And You Will Learn To:

Recording Video Demos

When you record screen actions using one of Captivate's automatic recording modes (such as the Custom mode you used beginning on page 4), mouse clicks result in screen captures. However, if you need to capture complex procedures like scrolling, drawing, moving, or resizing an object or dialog box, you can create a Video Demo. When you record a Video Demo, instead of creating individual slides for mouse clicks, Captivate creates one, seamless video.

The editing capabilities of a Video Demo are more limited than what you find within a standard Captivate project (where you edit one slide at a time, and each slide has its own Timeline). In a Video Demo there aren't any slides. There's a Timeline... but just one Timeline and it contains the entire video. You can add several standard Captivate objects to a Video Demo including text captions, highlight boxes, smart shapes, images, animations, and Characters. Sadly, you cannot add interactivity or quizzes to Video Demos (wave goodbye to such interactive favorites as click boxes, learner interactions, buttons, and text entry boxes). And while you cannot import standard Captivate projects into a Video Demo, you can import a Video Demo into a standard Captivate project (via **Insert > CPVC Slide**).

Student Activity: Record a Video Demo

1. Ensure that Captivate is running (no projects need to be open).

2. Set Captivate's Video Demo Preferences.

   ❑ Windows users, choose **Edit > Preferences**;
   Mac users, choose **Adobe Captivate > Preferences**

   ❑ from the **Recording** category, click **Video Demo**

   ❑ ensure that your options match the picture below (with the exception of the Working Folder because the information in that field varies from computer to computer)

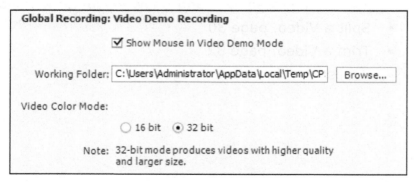

By selecting **Show Mouse in Video Demo Mode**, the video you record includes your mouse pointer in recorded video.

Videos created using **32 bit Video Color Mode** typically result in a larger video when compared to 16 bit videos. Although larger in file size than 16 bit videos, they'll look awesome. As you become more comfortable recording in Video Mode, experiment with the quality you get using both options. In the end, you should use the option that yields the best results for you.

   ❑ click the **OK** button

Note: You are about to use your web browser to visit the Disney site. The Disney home page may feature videos complete with music and other loud sound effects. If you are in an office setting, consider lowering the volume on your computer before going on the next step.

3. Rehearse the lesson you are going to record.

   ❑ using the web browser, go to **http://www.disney.com**

   Like many commercial websites, the Disney home page is very long. You will not be able to use Captivate or any screen capture utility to capture the entire page. Instead, you will record a Video Demo that scrolls around the Disney home page and highlights some of the many features on the site.

   ❑ at the right side of the browser window, drag the scroll bar **down** a few inches and then release your mouse

   ❑ drag the scroll bar **down** another few inches and then release your mouse

   ❑ drag the scroll back to the top of the page

   And that's it. At this point, you will stop the recording process. Let's return to Captivate and record the same actions using Video Mode.

4. Display the recording control panel.

   ❑ switch back to Captivate

   ❑ choose **File > Record a new > Video Demo**

   Just like recording a Software Simulation (see page 4), the main Captivate interface hides and the recording features open.

5. Select the browser window as the Application.

   ❑ from the top of the control panel, select **Application**

   ❑ from the drop-down menu that appears beneath Application, select the browser application you used to go to the Disney website

   ○ Screen Area ● Application

   🌐 Safari – Disney.com | The official home fo...   ▼

6. Specify a recording size.

   ❑ from the **Snap to** area, select **Custom Size**

   ❑ from the next drop-down menu, select **1024 x 576**

   Snap to
   ○ Application window   ○ Application Region   ● Custom Size
   1024 x 576   ▼
   1024   576

7. Disable Panning and Audio Narration.

   ❏ ensure that **Panning** is set to **No Panning** and that **Audio** is set to **No Narration**

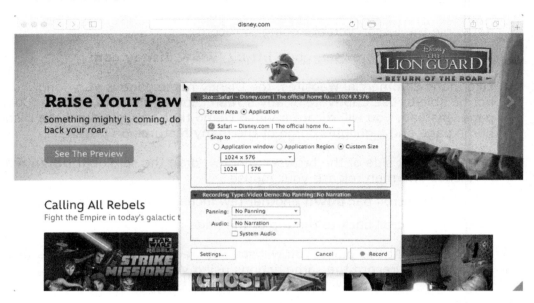

8. Record the Video Demo.

   ❏ click the **Record** button and wait for the countdown to go away

   ❏ at the right side of the browser window, drag the scroll bar **down** a few inches, and then release your mouse

   ❏ drag the scroll bar **down** another few inches and then release your mouse

   ❏ drag the scroll back to the top of the page

9. Stop the recording process and preview the video. (Use the Stop Recording key you set up on page 5.)

   Note: As mentioned during the previous module, if you can't get Captivate to stop recording via your keyboard shortcut, you can always manually stop the recording process by clicking the Captivate icon in the System Tray (Windows users) or the Dock (Mac users).

Once you stop the Recording process, you are returned to Captivate, and the lesson automatically plays within a Full Screen Preview. If you are a seasoned developer in Captivate, you will find this behavior a bit strange. When you end the recording process in every other mode, you are taken into Captivate's main interface where you would produce the lesson. You could preview the lesson at regular intervals along the way, but previewing is a process you need to initiate. With Video Demos, the first thing you do is preview the recording and then edit the video as needed.

10. Enter Video Edit mode.

☐ from the lower, right of the Preview window, click the **Edit** button

Once again, if you've spent any amount of time working within Captivate, things may seem a bit strange. For instance, there isn't a Filmstrip at the left. If you click Properties at the far right of the window, you will see that there is a new panel: the **Video Effects Inspector** with three tabs (Pan & Zoom, Popup, and Transitions). Notice also that the untitled video has a unique extension. Standard Captivate projects use a **cptx** extension. Video projects contain a **cpvc** extension, which stands for Captivate Video Composition.

11. Save the video project to the **Captivate9BeyondData** folder as **ScrollingDisney** and then close it. (You can also close the web browser containing the Disney website.)

Zooming and Panning

Captivate's Pan & Zoom feature is really two cool tools in one. Zooming gives you the ability to automatically get the learner closer to the action. Panning lets you automatically change the area of the screen that the learner sees.

Student Activity: Add a Video Zoom

1. Using Captivate, open the **PanZoomMe** video project from the Captivate9BeyondData folder.

2. Preview the video.

   ❏ choose **Preview > Project**

   This video demonstrates how to change both the Font and the Font Size in Microsoft Notepad. You are going to use the Pan & Zoom feature to move learners closer to the action.

   ❏ press [**esc**] to close the preview

3. Add a Pan & Zoom point to the Timeline.

   ❏ on the Timeline, click on the **2**-second mark

   The Playhead (the red bar) should be lined up at the 2-second mark on the Timeline. This is the part of the video where the Format menu is just about to be clicked.

   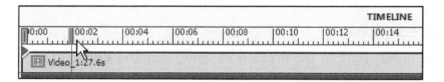

   ❏ choose **Window > Video Effects**

   The Video Effects Inspector opens at the right of the Captivate window. There are three tabs: Pan & Zoom, Popup, and Transitions. (If the Video Effects Inspector is not on your screen, choose **Window > Video Effects** again)

   ❏ on the **Video Effects** Inspector, select the **Pan & Zoom** tab
   ❏ click the **Add Pan & Zoom** button

   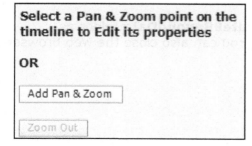

On the Timeline, a Pan & Zoom marker has been added (it's the orange circle with a magnifying glass in the middle).

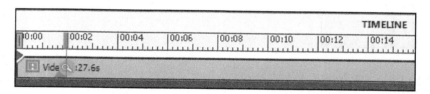

4. Change the Scale of the zoom.

   ☐ on the **Pan & Zoom** tab, change the Scale to **200** and press [**enter**]

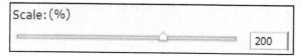

Notice two things. On the slide itself, you are much, much closer to the Notepad menus. On the Pan & Zoom tab, you can see the area targeted by the zoom.

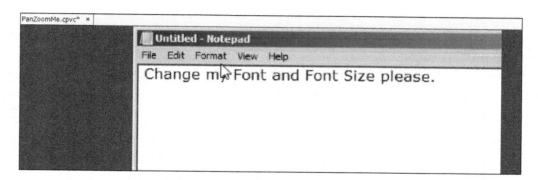

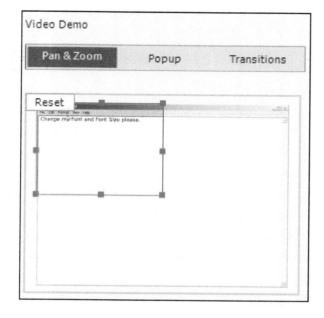

5. On the Timeline, drag the Playhead left to the beginning of the Timeline.

6. Preview the video (Preview > Project).

At the 2-second mark, you are automatically zoomed closer to Notepad's Format menu. Zooming closer to the action is an awesome feature. But there's a problem. You've zoomed very close to the action. However, you cannot see the font and font size being changed. You'll take care of that problem next by adding a second Pan & Zoom point on the Timeline and Panning across the video.

7. Close the Preview.

❒ click the **Edit** button in the lower right of the Preview window

Student Activity: Add a Video Pan

1. Ensure that the **PanZoomMe** video project is still open.

2. Add a second Pan & Zoom point to the Timeline.

   ☐ on the Timeline, click on the **5.7**-second mark

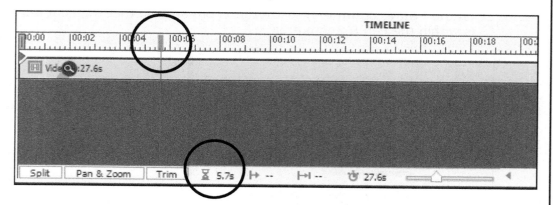

The Playhead (the red bar) should be lined up at the 5.7-second mark on the Timeline. This is the part of the video where Notepad's Font dialog box opens. You can tell that you've positioned the Playhead at the 5.7-second mark by observing the number at the right of the hourglass icon on the Timeline.

   ☐ on the **Pan & Zoom** tab, click the **Add Pan & Zoom** button

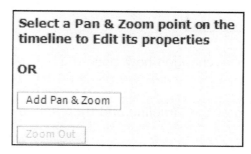

On the Timeline, notice that a second Pan & Zoom marker has been added.

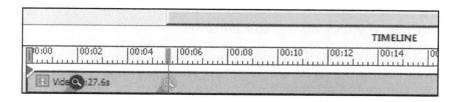

On the Pan & Zoom tab, notice that the Zoom scale and position is identical to what you created with the first Pan & Zoom marker. As you add more and more points along the Timeline, the new points always retain the attributes of the previous point.

3. Pan the video.

❒ on the **Pan & Zoom** tab, drag the Pan & Zoom area down and to the right so that it is centered over the Font dialog box

By dragging the Pan & Zoom area, you've panned the screen and changed what the learners see when they watch the demo.

❒ on the **Pan & Zoom** tab, resize the Zoom area so that the Font dialog box is within the Pan & Zoom area

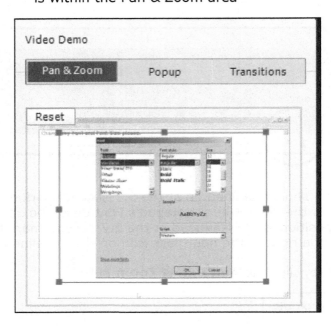

By resizing the Pan & Zoom area, you've changed how close the learners are to the video.

4. Position the Playhead at the beginning of the Timeline and then Preview the video.

At the 2-second mark, you are automatically zoomed closer to Notepad's Format menu. Next you pan right and can see what's happening within the Font dialog box. Awesome!

5. Close the Preview (by clicking the Edit button).

Note: You can remove a Pan & Zoom point from the Timeline at any time by right-clicking the point and choosing **Remove Pan & Zoom**. And you can change the attributes of any Pan & Zoom by selecting the Pan & Zoom point on the Timeline and editing the options as appropriate via the Pan & Zoom tab.

Pan & Zoom Confidence Check

1. Ensure that the **PanZoomMe** video project is still open.

2. On the Timeline, click at the **25.5**-second mark. (This is where the OK button is clicked in the Font dialog box.)

3. On the Pan & Zoom tab, click the **Zoom Out** button to instantly resize the Zoom Area (so that learners can see the entire Notepad window).

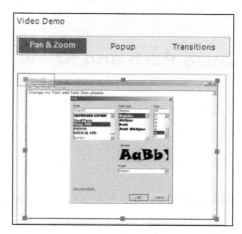

4. Preview from the beginning of the video to see the three Pan & Zooms that have been added to the video.

   Now you'll get a chance to add a transition to the beginning and end of the video.

5. On the left of the Timeline, select the **icon** that looks like one-half of a diamond. (This is one of two Transition Markers you have in the video... the other marker is on the right side of the Timeline.)

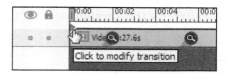

   On the Video Effects Inspector, notice that there is a **Transitions** tab.

6. Select any of the Transitions that you like; then click the half diamond at the right and add a Transition to the end of the video.

7. At the right of the Timeline, drag the **yellow rectangle** a bit to the right to extend the playtime for the video by a second or so.

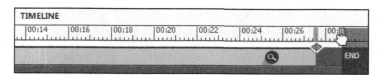

8. Preview from the beginning of the video to see the new Transition effects.

9. Save your work. Keep the project open for the next activity.

Mouse Points

If you had recorded a software Demonstration, the project you created would have included a mouse pointer on every slide that can easily be edited (the pointer can be moved or deleted, and its appearance, changed). Unfortunately, the project you are working with is a video. You can see the mouse pointer moving around the screen, but you cannot edit it. Or can you? Although it is not obvious that you have any mouse editing features in a Video Demo, looks are deceiving. In fact, you can display the mouse points within a Video Demo and perform such feats as deleting a mouse point, changing the appearance of the mouse, smoothing out the mouse path, and adding visual mouse clicks.

Student Activity: Smooth a Mouse Path and Show Visual Clicks

1. Ensure that the **PanZoomMe** video project is still open.

2. Display the Mouse Points.

   ❏ choose **Edit > Edit Mouse Points**

   On the Timeline, several mouse points appear. Each of the mouse points can be selected and edited.

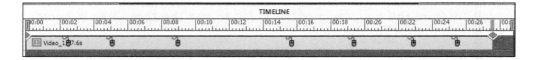

3. Smoothen a Mouse Path.

   ❏ on the Timeline, select the first mouse point

   On the video, notice that the mouse path begins in the middle of the screen and moves to the Format menu. The path taken by the mouse isn't as smooth as it could be. You'll fix that next.

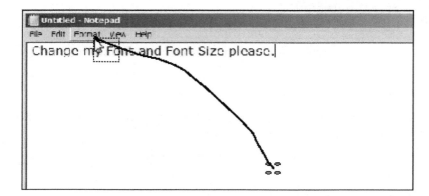

   ❏ on the Properties Inspector, select **Smoothen Mouse Path**

   ☑ *Smoothen Mouse Path

On the screen, notice that the appearance of the mouse path has gone from a jagged path to a smooth curve.

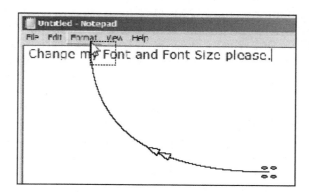

4. Show the Mouse Click.

   ❑ with the first mouse point still selected, select **Show Mouse Click** from the Properties Inspector

   ❑ from the drop-down menu below **Show Mouse Click**, choose **Custom**

   ❑ from the next drop-down menu, choose any of the animations (you can preview the animation by clicking the Play button to the right of the drop-down menu)

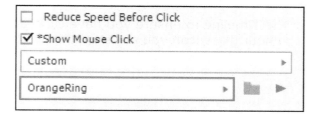

5. Preview from the beginning of the video to see the new mouse path and visual click.

6. Save and close the project.

Splitting

You have now learned how to create a Video Demo (page 18), how to use Pan and Zoom (page 22), and how to add Transitions (page 27). One limitation of Transitions is that you can add a Transition only to Transition Markers (the diamonds you see at the beginning and end of every video). But what if you need to add a Transition to the middle of a video segment? That's the perfect case for Splitting a single video into multiple pieces.

Student Activity: Split a Video

1. Open the **SplitMe** video project from the Captivate9BeyondData folder.

2. Preview the Project.

   This video demonstrates two Notepad concepts: how to cut and paste text and how to change the Font and Font Size of text. Your goal is to add a transition between the first and second parts of the lesson. (Transitions have already been added to the beginning and end of the video.)

   ❐ click the **Edit** button to close the preview

3. Split the video into two segments.

   ❐ on the Timeline, click on the **25.0**-second mark

   Once again, use the bottom of the Timeline to ensure you have clicked in the correct part of the Timeline. The hour glass icon you see should have 25.0s just to the right.

   ❐ on the bottom left of the Timeline, click the **Split** button

   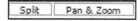

   On the Timeline, notice that the video has been split into two segments and that there is a Transition Marker between the two segments.

4. Save your work.

Transitions Confidence Check

1. Ensure that the **SplitMe** video project is still open.

2. Add any Transition you like to the new Transition Marker. Need help? See page 27.

3. Preview the video from the beginning to see the new Transition effect.

4. Save and close the project.

Trimming

During the recording process, every recording misstep or delay shows up in a Video Demo. For instance, if you intend to show the process of accessing the File menu in an application and accidentally open a different menu, the gaffe is recorded. The same is true if you begin the recording process but take several seconds to move your mouse. Every second and everything you do is being recorded. If you've recorded some missteps, you'll find the Trim feature in Captivate invaluable.

Student Activity: Trim a Video

1. Open the **TrimMe** video project from the Captivate9BeyondData folder.

2. Preview the video.

   This video is similar to the other videos you have played with during this module. However, there is a significant amount of time at the beginning of the video where the mouse is just moving around the screen and nothing of substance is being demonstrated. You'll trim out that part of the video next.

3. Trim out the first few seconds of the video.

   ☐ close the preview

   ☐ on the Timeline, ensure the red playhead is located at the far **left** (the beginning of the video)

   ☐ slowly drag the playhead **right** along the Timeline

   As you drag the playhead, you can see the mouse moving around but not really accomplishing anything. The first six seconds of the video need to go.

   ☐ position the playhead on the Timeline at **6** seconds

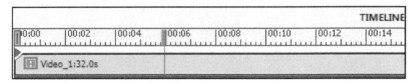

   ☐ at the bottom of the Timeline, click the **Trim** button

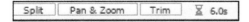

   On the Timeline, **Trim Begin** ◥ and **Trim End** ◤ markers appear on either side of the playhead.

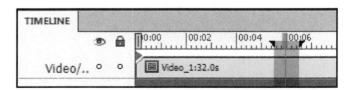

   ☐ drag the **Trim Begin** marker all the way to the **left**

❑ drag the **Trim End** marker just a bit left so that it is lined up with the playhead at **6** seconds

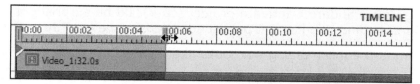

❑ at the bottom of the Timeline, click **Trim**

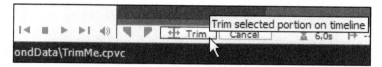

And like magic, the unwanted (selected) portion of the video is gone.

Trimming Confidence Check

1. Ensure that the **TrimMe** video project is still open.

2. The last few seconds of the video need to be trimmed. Go ahead and make it happen.

3. Preview from the beginning of the video to see the newly trimmed video.

4. Save and close the project.

Publishing Video Projects

Publishing a Video Demo (cpvc) might seem like a no-brainer if you have past experience working with standard Captivate project (cptx). I'd be surprised if any Captivate developers reading this haven't published at least once via **File > Publish**.

Here's what the standard Publish dialog box looks like:

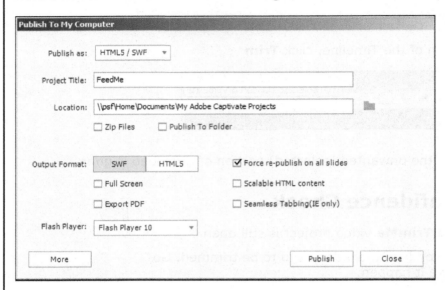

When publishing a cptx project, you can output an SWF, HTML5, PDF, or all of the above. You can also publish as a video file. The bottom line is that you have choices... lots of choices.

Publishing a Video Demo is, to put it mildly, different. As with a cptx project, you still choose **File > Publish**. However, the Publish dialog box that appears doesn't contain many options:

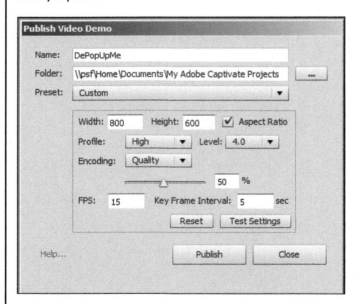

SWF? Gone. HTML5? PDF? Gone and gone! If you're working with a Video Demo and go to publish, the assumption is that you want to publish, well, a video. And that's exactly what you get when you publish—an MP4 file that plays nicely on YouTube and just about any computer or mobile device that supports videos.

Here are a few things to keep in mind when customizing the settings in the Publish dialog box.

Profile: There are three choices (Baseline, Main, and High). Baseline is for mobile and video conferencing applications. Main is for standard-definition digital TV broadcasts. High is for high definition devices. Although the High Profile leads to a longer publish time and more complex video, I've found that this option yields the best results.

Encoding: Constant (CBR) is the default (and it's what I use 99.99% of the time). A Constant bit rate typically results in a smaller published video. A Variable (VBR) bit rate results in Captivate deciding when to use more bits to maintain quality. The file size increases when more bits are used.

FPS stands for Frames Per Second. The higher the value, the smoother your video will play, and the larger the published video will be. The standard FPS is 15.

Key Frame Interval: All videos contain key frames (milestones that represent every second of playtime for the video). The longer you set the Key Frame Interval, the smaller the published video file will be.

Student Activity: Publish a Video Demo

1. Open the **PublishMe** video project from the **Captivate9BeyondData** folder.

2. Publish a video.

   ❏ choose **File > Publish**

   The Publish Video Demo dialog box opens.

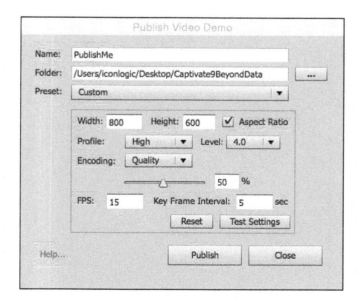

   ❏ to the right of **Folder**, click the **Browse** button (the three dots)
   ❏ open the **Captivate9BeyondData** folder
   ❏ from the bottom of the dialog box, click the **Reset** button

Any changes that you might have made to the video settings are returned to their default values. I almost always publish my videos using the default values.

❏ click the **Publish** button

Once the project has been published, the Video dialog box opens.

❏ click the **Open Published Video** button

The published MP4 video open in your default video player.

3. Close the video.

4. Click the Close button to close the Video dialog box.

5. Save and close the video project.

iCONLOGiC

"Skills and Drills" Learning

Module 3: Branching and Aggregating

In This Module You Will Learn About:

And You Will Learn To:

Object Styles

It might be an understatement, but consistency among slides in a project (and from project to project) is important. Few things lower the professional look and feel of a project or course than dissimilar slide objects, such as the haphazard use of fonts, sizes, and colors. Fortunately, you can elect to apply Object Styles that ship with Captivate to just about any slide object. Object Styles contain myriad formatting options designed to ensure that slide objects are formatted consistently. If you need to follow your own corporate standards and style guide, you can create your own custom Object Styles.

Student Activity: Create a New Style

1. Open **RenameFolder** from the Captivate9BeyondData folder.

2. Preview the project.

   This is a nine-slide project complete with images, captions, and highlight boxes. You'll soon be adding the slides and objects in this project to another Captivate project.

   As you watch the preview, pay particular attention to the appearance of the project's text captions. The Caption Type is **HaloRed**, and the font is Times New Roman. Simply put, this project's formatting needs some work.

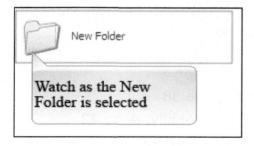

3. Close the preview.

4. Close the project (do not save the project if prompted).

5. Open **FeedMe** from the Captivate9BeyondData folder.

6. Save the project to the Captivate9BeyondData folder as **CreatingRenamingFolders**.

7. Preview the project.

   This nine-slide project contains text captions that already look much better than those in the RenameFolder project. You are going to make some slight changes to one of the text captions and save those changes as a custom style.

8. Close the preview.

9. Reset an Object Style.

   ☐ go to slide **8**

   ☐ select the **Text Caption**

   Observe the top of the **Properties Inspector**. The selected caption was originally using the Default Caption Style. At some point, it was manually formatted using some of the formatting options on the Properties Inspector. You can tell that an object was manually formatted by the **plus sign** that appears to the left of the style's name in the **Style Name** drop-down menu.

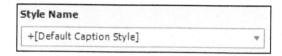

   There is nothing wrong with manually formatting slide objects. However, using Object Styles is helpful in ensuring that objects in a project are consistently formatted.

   ☐ on the **Properties Inspector**, click the menu to the right of **Style Name** and choose **Reset Style**

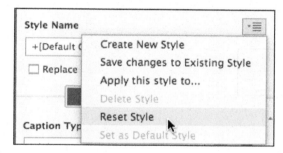

   Selecting Reset Style removes all of the manual formatting applied to the selected caption. The caption should now look like the other text captions in the project.

10. Change the properties of a text caption.

    ☐ go to another slide and select any text caption

    On the Properties Inspector, notice that the selected text caption is using the Default Caption Style. There's no plus sign, so the object is using the Object Style without any overrides.

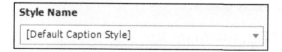

❏ on the Properties Inspector, select the **Style** tab

❏ from the **Caption Type** drop-down menu, choose **Frosted**

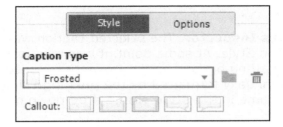

❏ from the **Character** area, change the Font Size to **14**

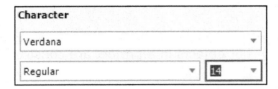

On the Properties Inspector, notice that the Default Caption Style has a plus sign to the left of the style name. The plus sign is an indication of a style override.

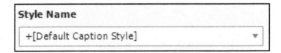

11. Create a new style.

❏ on the **Properties Inspector**, click the menu to the right of **Style Name** and choose **Create New Style**

The Save New Object Style dialog box opens.

❏ name the new Object Style: **SSS_TextCaptions**

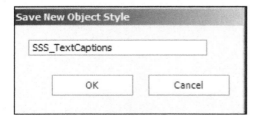

❐ click the **OK** button

The new style is immediately applied to the text caption you modified.
In addition, the style appears in the Style drop-down menu on the Properties
Inspector.

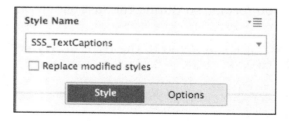

12. Save your work.

Student Activity: Apply an Object Style Globally

1. Ensure that the **CreatingRenamingFolders** project is still open.

2. Apply the new text caption style to all of the project's text captions.

   ❏ ensure that the text caption you formatted during the last activity is selected

   ❏ on the **Properties Inspector**, click the menu to the right of **Style Name** and choose **Apply this style to**

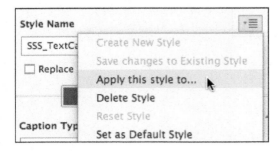

The Apply Object Style dialog box opens.

   ❏ ensure that **Default Caption Style** appears in the drop-down menu

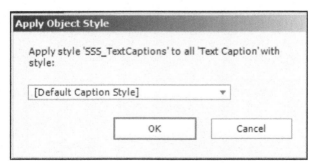

   ❏ click the **OK** button

Because all of the text captions in the project are using the Default Caption Style (except the one caption that you reformatted), every text caption in the project is now using the new SSS_TextCaptions style.

3. Save your work.

Sharing Styles

When you edit or create Object Styles within one Captivate project, those changes do not appear in other projects. If you would like to share Object Styles with fellow Captivate developers or use Object Styles created by another developer in your project, Captivate's ability to both import and export styles is an invaluable feature.

Student Activity: Export/Import a Style

1. Ensure that the **CreatingRenamingFolders** project is still open.

2. Export a style.

   ❑ choose **Edit > Object Style Manager**

   The Object Style Manager dialog box opens.

   ❑ from the top center of the dialog box, select the **SSS_TextCaptions** style you created earlier

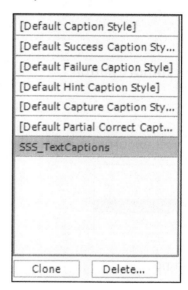

   [Default Caption Style]

   [Default Success Caption Sty...]

   [Default Failure Caption Style]

   [Default Hint Caption Style]

   [Default Capture Caption Sty...]

   [Default Partial Correct Capt...]

   SSS_TextCaptions

   Clone   Delete...

   ❑ from the bottom of the dialog box, click the drop-down menu between the **Import** and **Export** buttons

   ❑ if necessary, select **Selected style only**

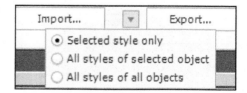

   Import...   ▼   Export...

   ⦿ Selected style only

   ◯ All styles of selected object

   ◯ All styles of all objects

   ❑ click the **Export** button

   ❑ confirm that the name of the file to be exported is **SSS_TextCaptions.cps** and then **save** the file to the **Captivate9BeyondData** folder

❑ click the **OK** button to acknowledge the successful export

❑ click the **OK** button to close the Object Style Manager dialog box

3. Save your work (leave the CreatingRenamingFolders project open).

4. Reopen the **RenameFolder** project from the Captivate9BeyondData folder.

5. Go to slide **2** and notice once again that the caption style and font used does not match the CreatingRenamingFolders project.

6. Import an Object Style.

❑ choose **Edit > Object Style Manager**

❑ from the bottom of the dialog box, click the **Import** button

❑ open the **SSS_TextCaptions.cps** file that you exported a moment ago

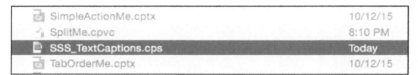

You will be asked if you want to overwrite existing styles.

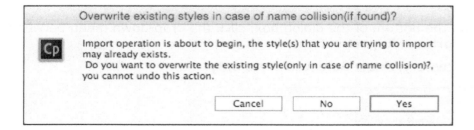

❑ click the **Yes** button

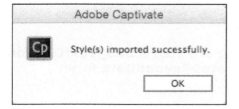

❏ click the **OK** button to acknowledge the successful import

The imported style appears in the list in the middle of the dialog box. You will use the imported style during the Confidence Check that follows.

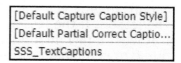

❏ click the **OK** button to close the Object Style Manager dialog box

Styles Confidence Check

1. Still working in the **RenameFolder** project, select the text caption on slide 2.

2. Use the Properties Inspector to apply the imported **SSS_TextCaptions** style to the caption.

3. Use the **Apply this style to** command to apply the **SSS_TextCaptions** to all of the project's text captions that are using the Default Caption Style. (You learned how to do this on page 42.)

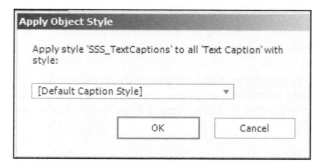

4. Save your work. (Keep the project open.)

Combining Projects

The ideal play time for published Captivate lessons is approximately five minutes. A lesson that plays much longer runs the risk of losing the learner, thanks to any number of distractions prevalent in today's hectic world. On the other hand, shorter isn't necessarily better. If the lesson doesn't contain enough "meat," you will likely find that your learners resent that you had them start the lesson. If the lesson doesn't contain enough slides to engage the learner for at least a few minutes, you should consider either not including the lesson in the course or combining the lesson with another lesson. The two projects that you have been playing with over the past few activities (CreatingRenamingFolders and RenameFolder) are both very short. In the next activity, you'll combine them into one project.

Student Activity: Name a Slide

1. Ensure that both the **CreatingRenamingFolders** and **RenameFolder** projects are open.

2. Switch to the **CreatingRenamingFolders** project. (You can click the project's tab to make it the active project.)

3. Add a Name to a slide.

   ❑ on the Filmstrip, select slide **1**

   ❑ from the top of the **Properties Inspector**, type **Lesson 1: Create New Folder** into the field and press [**enter**] on your keyboard

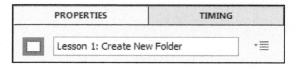

The new name appears below the thumbnail of the slide on the Filmstrip. The slide name proves useful when you are pasting content from one project into another and when you are creating a branch. You will perform both tasks shortly.

4. Save your work.

Naming Slides Confidence Check

1. Name the last slide in the **CreatingRenamingFolders** project as **End Lesson 1**.

2. Switch to the **RenameFolder** project and name the first slide **Lesson 2: Renaming Folders**.

3. Name the next to last slide **End Lesson 2** and the last slide **Congrats**.

4. Open the **TOCSlide** project from the Captivate9BeyondData folder and name the only slide in the project **TOC**.

5. Save all three of the open projects (**File > Save All**).

Student Activity: Copy/Paste Project Assets

1. Ensure that the **CreatingRenamingFolders**, **RenameFolder**, and **TOCSlide** projects are all still open.

2. Copy slides and objects from the RenameFolder project to the clipboard.

   ❏ switch to the **RenameFolder** project and on the Filmstrip, select slide **1**

   ❏ scroll down to the bottom of the Filmstrip, press [**Shift**] on your keyboard, and then select the last slide (Slide 9, the Congrats slide)

   ❏ release the [**Shift**] key

   ❏ choose **Edit > Copy** to copy the selected slides to the clipboard

3. Paste the slides from the clipboard into the another project.

   ❏ switch to the **CreatingRenamingFolders** project

   ❏ scroll down the Filmstrip and select the **last slide** (the End Lesson 1 slide)

   ❏ choose **Edit > Paste**

   And just like that, the assets from the RenameFolder project have been added to the CreatingRenamingFolders project (slides, slide objects, slide names, etc.). The CreatingRenamingFolders project now consists of 18 slides.

4. Copy and paste the assets from the TOCSlide project into the CreatingRenamingFolders project.

   ❏ switch to the **TOCSlide** project

   ❏ choose **Edit > Copy** to copy the project's only slide to the clipboard

   ❏ switch to the **CreatingRenamingFolders** project, select the **first slide** in the project, and then choose **Edit > Paste**

   The newly pasted TOC slide is the second slide on the Filmstrip.

   ❏ on the Filmstrip, drag the **TOC** slide into the first position

5. Save and close all of the projects.

Branching

The **CreatingRenamingFolders** project you worked with during the past few activities contains two distinct lessons: **Creating New Folders** and **Renaming Folders**. You combined the two lessons into one course when you copied the assets from the RenameFolder project into the CreatingRenamingFolders project. The first slide in the project is a menu that gives learners access to either section. When you allow learners to choose multiple paths in a lesson, you've created a branch. Because you can have multiple branches in a project, you will appreciate Captivate's Navigation workspace, which provides an overview of where the branches go and what the learner needs to click to follow the branch.

Student Activity: Use Buttons to Create a Branch

1. Open the **BranchMe** project from the Captivate9BeyondData folder.

   This project is identical to the completed CreatingRenamingFolders project you were working with during the last activity.

   On slide **1** (the TOC slide) notice that there are two buttons on the slide, one for each part of the lesson (Create New Folders and Rename Folders).

2. Set the action for a button to jump to a specific slide in the project.

   ☐ on slide **1**, double-click the **Create New Folders** button to open the Properties Inspector

   Note: If you see only the Timing Inspector at the right of the Captivate window (instead of both Properties and Timing), close and then reopen the Properties Inspector.

   ☐ on the Properties Inspector, select the **Actions** tab

   ☐ from the **On Success** drop-down menu, choose **Jump to slide**

   ☐ from the **Slide** drop-down menu, ensure **2 Lesson 1: Create New Folder** is selected

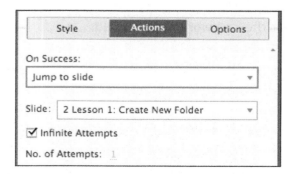

Branching Confidence Check

1. Still working within the **BranchMe** project, set the button Action for the **Rename Folders** button so that it jumps to slide **11, Lesson 2: Renaming Folders**.

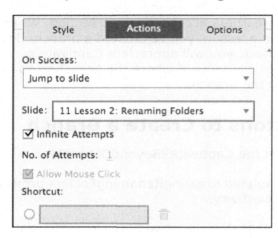

2. Save your work and preview the project.

3. Click the buttons and ensure that their Actions work as expected (the buttons should branch you to either slide **2** or **11**).

4. Close the Preview.

5. On slide **2**, set the properties for the three buttons as follows:

   ❐ **Play Lesson:** Go to the next slide

   ❐ **Home:** Jumps to slide **1** (TOC)

   ❐ **Next Lesson:** Jumps to slide **11**, Lesson 2: Renaming Folders

6. On slide **11**, set the properties for the three buttons as follows:

   ❐ **Play Lesson:** Go to the next slide

   ❐ **Home:** Jumps to slide **1** (TOC)

   ❐ **Previous Lesson:** Jumps to slide **2**, Lesson 1: Create New Folder

7. On the last slide, set the properties for the two buttons as follows:

   ❐ **Create New Folders:** Jumps to slide **2**, Lesson 1: Create New Folder

   ❐ **Rename Folders:** Jumps to slide **11**, Lesson 2: Renaming Folders

8. Save your work and preview the project.

9. Click the buttons and ensure that they all work as expected.

10. Close the Preview.

11. Close the Project.

Student Activity: Explore the Branching View

1. Open the **NavigateMe** project from the Captivate9BeyondData folder.

2. View the Branching window.

   ☐ **Window > Branching View**

   The Branching window opens. The window is split into two main sections. At the top you see the individual branches you set up when you created Actions for several buttons on the slides. The bottom panel contains an orange box that allows you to scroll through a long branch.

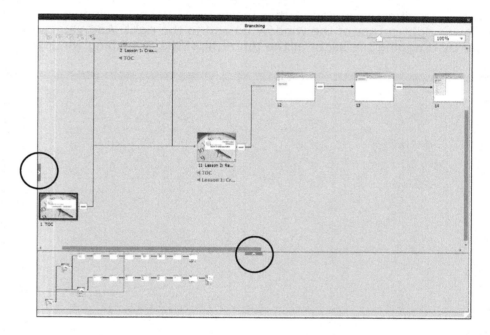

There are also two **Splitter Bars** (shown below and circled in the image above), one at the far left and another at the bottom center.

☐ click the Splitter Bar at the **left** of the Branching window

You expose a third panel (Legends). The color of the arrows you might see in the main Navigation panel are explained in the Legend.

☐ click the Splitter bar at the **bottom**

You either expand or collapse a panel containing the orange box. You can play with the orange box as you see fit. Try dragging it left or right and notice that doing so allows you to scroll through the branching view above.

3. Click both Splitter Bars as necessary to collapse both the panel at the left and the panel at the bottom.

4. Zoom away from the Navigation panel.

   ❏ from the top right of the Branching window, change the magnification to **Best Fit**

You should now be able to clearly see the branches you created during the previous activities. (You can further resize the Branching window by dragging the lower right corner of the window up and to the right. And you can zoom closer by dragging the slider at the top right of the Branching window.)

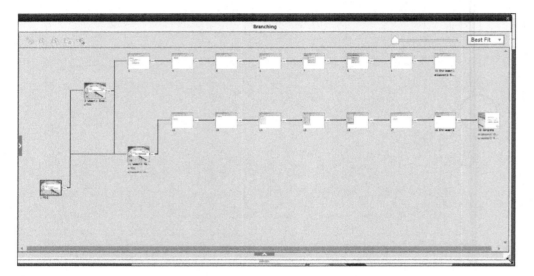

5. Explore the Action properties of a branch.

   ❏ on the Branching window, zoom in just enough so you can clearly see the green arrow to the left of slide **3**

   ❏ on the Branching window, click the arrow to the left of slide **3**

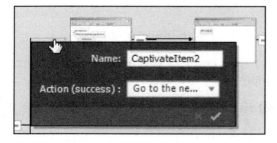

Information about the button's Action appears. You could easily change the Action here instead of opening the slide and showing the Properties of the button—a huge time-saver.

   ❏ at the bottom of the information window, click the red **X** to close the Action properties

6. Export the Branching view as an image.

   ☐ at the top left of the Branching window, click the **Export Branching View** tool

   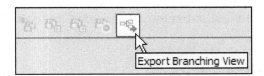

   The Export branching view dialog box appears.

   ☐ open the **Captivate9BeyondData** folder

   ☐ save the image as **CreateRename_BranchingView**

   ☐ select **Jpeg Files** from the **Save as type** area (Windows) or the **File Format** area (Mac) and then save the image

   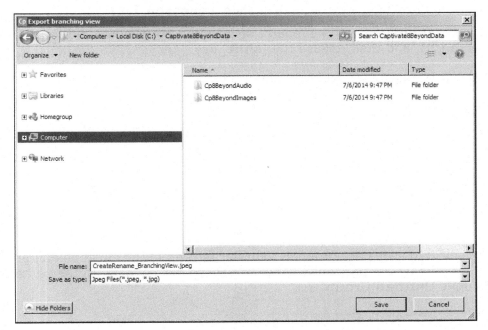

   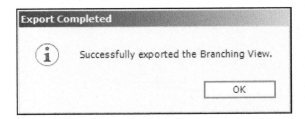

   ☐ click the **OK** button

   The image has been exported to the Captivate9BeyondData folder. You could now import the image into any program that accepts jpeg images. Or you could email the image to a team member or manager for review.

Groups

If your project is large and contains multiple branches, keeping track of the branches could become a nightmare. Slide groups allow you to group slides within a branch together, providing an excellent overview of the project. The groups you create can be expanded and collapsed, allowing you to view subsets of the slides instead of all slides at one time.

Student Activity: Create a Slide Group

1. Ensure that the **NavigateMe** project is still open and that the Branching window is still open.

2. Change the Branching window view to **Best Fit**.

3. Select a group of slides.

   ❐ in the Branching window, select slide **2 (Lesson 1...)**

   ❐ press [**shift**] on your keyboard, select slide **10** (the last slide in the branch), and then release the [**shift**] key

   Slides **2** through **10** should now be selected.

4. Create a Slide Group.

   ❐ on the Branching window, click the **Create Slide Group** tool

   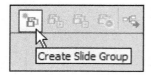

   The selected slides are grouped together (shown in the circle below) and no longer take up the horizontal space they once did. By default, the name of the group is **Untitled Group**.

   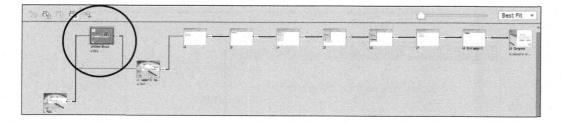

5. Title the new Slide Group.

   ❐ on the Properties Inspector, change the **Title** of the Group to **CreateNewFolder**

   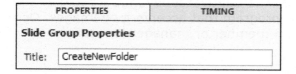

PROPERTIES	TIMING
Slide Group Properties	
Title: CreateNewFolder	

6. View expanding thumbnails of the new Slide Group.

   ❏ point to the middle of the slide group you just created

   The slides in the group open horizontally across the Branching window. When you move your mouse away from the group, the group collapses, once again saving horizontal space on the Branch panel.

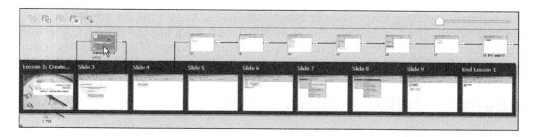

7. Explore the group on the Filmstrip.

   ❏ close the Branching window

   On the Filmstrip, notice that several slides appear to be missing.

   ❏ click the arrow at the upper left of the CreateNewFolder thumbnail

   The group expands revealing all of the slides in the group. You can click the arrow again to collapse the group.

8. Save and close the project.

Aggregating

It's a best practice to create lessons that a learner can finish within five minutes—which typically translates to 80-100 interactive slides. Of course, there may be occasions where you want to take several small projects and bring them together into one course without copying/pasting slides or objects from one project into another (as you learned to do earlier in this module).

If you publish multiple Captivate projects as SWFs, they can be added to an Aggregator project as modules. Once added to an Aggregator project, the combined modules can be published as a cohesive eLearning course. The published course will include a Table of Contents allowing learners to easily jump from module to module.

Student Activity: Publish SWFs

1. Publish a project as an SWF.

   ☐ open the **Introduction** project from the Captivate9BeyondData folder

   The Introduction project (as well as the remaining projects you will open in this module) was provided by **Next Turn Consulting**, a training company specializing in improving corporate communications.

   ☐ choose **File > Publish**

   ☐ from the **Publish as** drop-down menu, choose **HTML5/SWF**

   ☐ ensure that the **Project Title** is **Introduction**

   ☐ from the **Location** area, click the **Browse** button and open the **Captivate9BeyondData** folder

   ☐ select **Publish To Folder**

Publish as:	HTML5 / SWF ▾
Project Title:	Introduction
Location:	/Users/iconlogic/Desktop/Captivate9BeyondData
	☐ Zip Files ☑ Publish To Folder

   ☐ from the **Output Format** area, select **SWF**

Output Format:	SWF	HTML5

   ☐ from the **Flash Player Version** drop-down menu, ensure **Flash Player 10** is selected

Flash Player versions 10, 10.2, and 11 are available in the Flash Player Version drop-down menu. I recommend that you use Flash Player 10. If you select a newer version of the Flash Player (like 11), learners who still have an older Flash Player (and there are plenty of them out there) will not be able to view the published SWF.

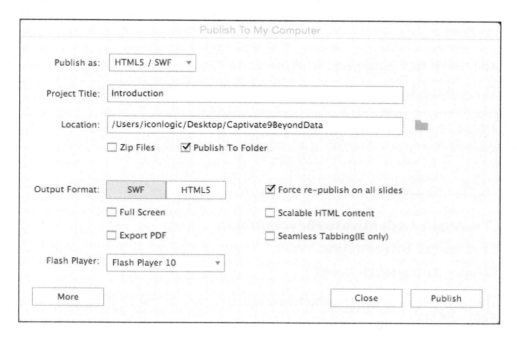

☐ click the **Publish** button

☐ click the **No** button when prompted to view the output

2. Save and close the project.

Publishing Confidence Check

There are two more projects needing to be published as SWFs so they can be used in the Aggregator.

1. Open **Module1** from the Captivate9BeyondData folder.

2. Publish the project within the Captivate9BeyondData folder as an SWF. Ensure that **Publish to Folder** is selected and that the Title of the lesson is **Module1**. Publish the SWF using Flash Player Version **10**. (There is no need to view the published project when prompted.)

3. Open **Module2** from the Captivate9BeyondData folder.

4. Publish the project within the Captivate9BeyondData folder as an SWF. Ensure that **Publish to Folder** is selected and that the Title of the lesson is **Module2**. Publish the SWF using Flash Player Version **10**. (There is no need to view the published project when prompted.)

5. Save and close all projects.

Student Activity: Aggregate SWFs

1. Create an Aggregator Project.

   ☐ choose **File > New Project > Aggregator Project**

   The Aggregator window opens, ready for you to add your published SWFs as modules.

2. Add SWFs to the Aggregator project.

   ☐ from the bottom of the Aggregator, click the **Add Module** tool

   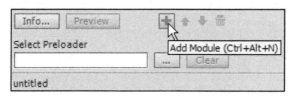

   ☐ navigate to **Captivate9BeyondData**
   ☐ open the **Introduction** folder
   ☐ open **Introduction.swf**

   The SWF you published a moment ago appears in the Module Title area of the Aggregator.

3. Save the Aggregator project.

   ☐ from the top of the Aggregator window, click the **Save Aggregator Project** tool

   ☐ save the Aggregator project to the **Captivate9BeyondData** data folder with the name **CalmInConflict**

   Note: Unlike Captivate projects, which use a **cptx** extension for standard projects and **cpvc** for video projects, Aggregator projects use an **aggr** extension.

Aggregator Confidence Check

1. Ensure that the **CalmInConflict** Aggregator project is still open.

2. Add **Module1** and **Module2** to the Aggregator project as modules.

3. Double-click the **Introduction** module and remove the .swf extension from its name.

4. Change the **Module1.swf** title to **Module 1**. (Remove the .swf from the title and put a space between the word "Module" and the "1.")

5. Change the **Module2.swf** title to **Module 2**. (Remove the .swf from the title and put a space between the word "Module" and the "2.")

6. Publish the project by clicking the **Publish Aggregator Project** tool at the top of the Aggregator window.

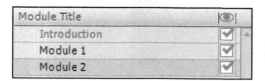

7. From the **Format** area, select **SWF**.

8. Ensure that the Title is **CalmInConflict**.

9. From the **Folder** area, browse to the **Captivate9BeyondData** folder.

10. From the **Publish Options** area, select **Export PDF**.

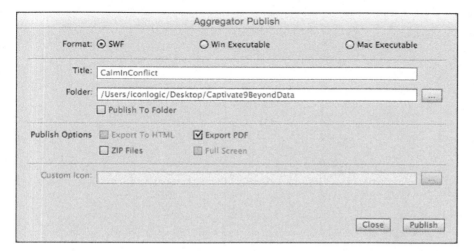

11. Click the Publish button and then click the **Yes** button to view the output.

12. If you have the latest Adobe Acrobat Reader and Flash Player on your computer, the aggregated PDF lessons open in either Reader or Acrobat. You can use the TOC at the left to jump between the lessons. Adobe PDFs are capable of playing rich media, such as audio and animation, and include interactivity. In a word... awesome!

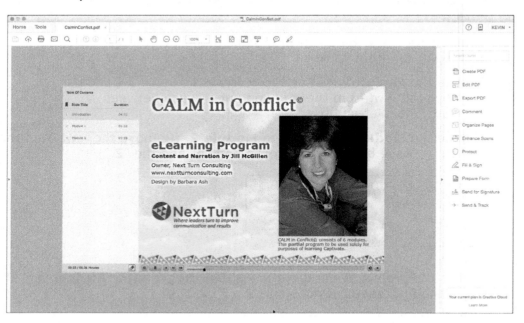

13. When finished previewing the output, close the PDF.

14. Save and close the Aggregator project.

iCONLOGiC

"Skills and Drills" Learning

Module 4: Random Quizzes

In This Module You Will Learn About:

- GIFT Files, page 62
- Question Pools, page 64
- Random Question Slides, page 68

And You Will Learn To:

- Review a GIFT File, page 62
- Import a GIFT File into a Project, page 63
- Create Question Pools, page 64
- Move Questions to Pools, page 66
- Insert Random Question Slides, page 68

GIFT Files

To add question slides to a Captivate project, you can visit the Quiz menu and choose Question Slide. You'll be presented with the Insert Questions dialog box giving you access to several types of questions you can add including Multiple Choice, True/False, and Matching. Once the questions have been added to your project, the next step is to edit the questions and answers. If you need to add a large number of question slides to a project, you will need an incredible amount of time to create the quiz.

There is a better way to go, especially if the person creating the quiz does not have or use Adobe Captivate... GIFT files. GIFT stands for General Import Format Technology. You can create a GIFT file in plain text using a simple word processor (like Notepad or TextEdit) and then import the file into Adobe Captivate.

Student Activity: Review a GIFT File

1. Minimize/Hide Adobe Captivate.

2. Using either Notepad (Windows) or TextEdit (Mac), open **GiftMe** from the Captivate9BeyondData folder.

   The GIFT file is a simple text file containing one multiple choice question. The syntax is simple. The Question Title goes between the double set of colons. Next comes the question itself. The answers are within the {}. The correct answer is preceded by an equal sign (=); the incorrect answers are preceded by a tilde (~).

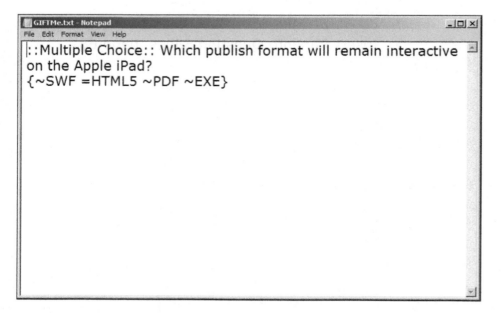

3. Close the GiftMe file (do not save any changes if prompted).

Student Activity: Import a GIFT File into a Project

1. Open **PoolMe** from the Captivate9BeyondData folder.

   The project contains a 19-question quiz made up of True/False and Multiple Choice questions. You will soon create three Question Pools that contribute to a random quiz. But first, let's add a new question slide using the GIFT file you just reviewed.

2. Import a GIFT file.

   ❑ ensure slide **1** is selected

   ❑ choose **Quiz > Import GIFT Format File**

   ❑ from the **Captivate9BeyondData** folder, open **GiftMe.txt**

   A multiple choice question is instantly added to the project after the selected slide 1.

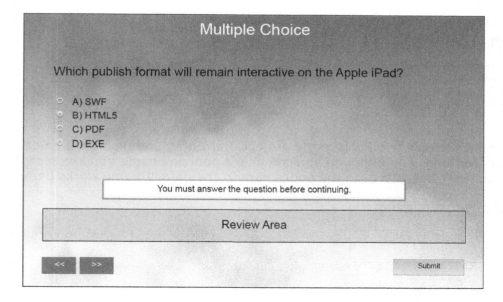

Question Pools

Creating a random quiz begins with Question Pools. Each Captivate project contains a single Question Pool (named Pool1). You can create as many pools as you need. The more Question Pools you have and the more question slides you have in each pool, the more random your quiz will be.

Student Activity: Create Question Pools

1. Ensure that the **PoolMe** project is still open.

2. Display the Question Pool Manager.

   ☐ choose **Quiz > Question Pool Manager**

   The Question Pool Manager dialog box opens. By default, there is one pool named **Pool1**.

3. Create a Question Pool.

   ☐ click the plus sign above the existing Pool1 Question Pool

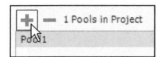

There are now two Pools in the project. Currently, both Pools are empty, but not for long. And although you can give a pool any name you like (as long as you don't use spaces in the pool's name), the default name works perfectly.

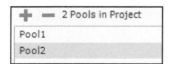

   ☐ click the **Close** button

Instead of seeing a slide in the middle of the screen, you see an Empty Question Pool. When you add question slides to the pools, this area of the Captivate window fills with content.

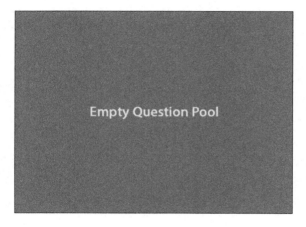

Question Pools Confidence Check

1. Ensure that the **PoolMe** project is still open.

2. Choose **Window > Question Pool**.

   The Question Pool panel appears at the bottom of the Captivate window. This area populates with questions as you move the project's question slides to the question pools.

3. The project's two Question Pools are empty (you can view each of your two pools via the drop-down menu at the right of the panel).

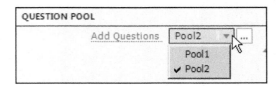

4. At the far right of Question Pool panel, click Question Pool Manager (the three dots).

5. Create a third Question Pool (click the **Close** button when finished).

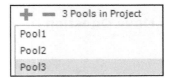

6. Save your work.

Student Activity: Move Questions to Pools

1. Ensure that the **PoolMe** project is still open.

2. Move a Question Slide to a Question Pool.

   ☐ on the Filmstrip, right-click slide **2** and choose **Move Question to > Pool1**

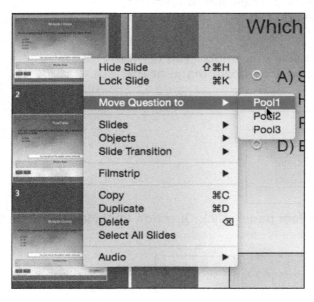

The slide disappears from the Filmstrip. No worries! It's safe and sound in the Pool1 pool (which you will see soon enough on the Question Pools panel).

3. Move another Question Slide to a Question Pool.

   ☐ on the Filmstrip, right-click slide **2** and choose **Move Question to > Pool2**

4. View Question Slides in their respective Pools.

   ☐ on the Question Pool panel, select **Pool1** and then **Pool2** from the drop-down menu to view the single Question Slide in each Pool

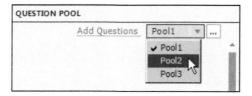

Moving Questions to Pools Confidence Check

On the Filmstrip, slides 2 through 19 are all Question Slides and need to be added to the Question Pools. (Slides 1 and 20 are not Question Slides, so you will not be able to accidentally add them to any of the Pools.)

1. Beginning with slide 2 on the Filmstrip, add the Question Slides to the Question Pools randomly or as you see fit.

2. Show the Question Pool Manager (Quiz menu).

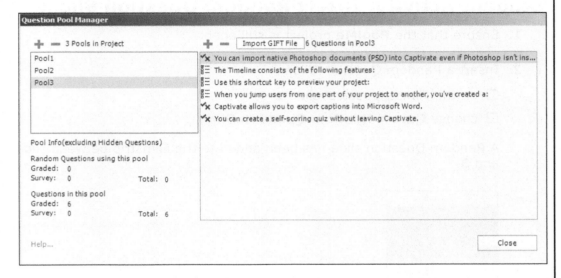

3. Select each of the Pools one by one and, from the information that appears at the left of the Question Pool Manager, notice how many questions are in each pool.

   If you would like to move a question from one pool to another, return to the Question Pool panel, right-click any question, and choose **Move Question to**.

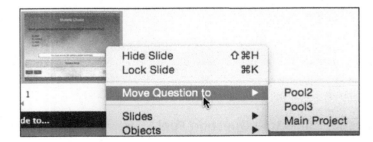

4. Close the Question Pools Manager.

5. Save your work.

Random Question Slides

Up to this point you've created Question Pools and moved all of the questions in the project to the pools. In the process, you've removed all of the slides from the Filmstrip. So how will Captivate serve up a random quiz to your learners if there aren't any questions on the Filmstrip to publish? The answer lies in a bit of brilliance devised by Adobe: Random Question Slides. You'll add some Random Question Slides to the Filmstrip to serve as proxies for the missing question slides. Because you can link each Random Question Slides to a Question Pool, a question is randomly selected from the pool and presented to the learner during the quiz.

Student Activity: Insert Random Question Slides

1. Ensure that the **PoolMe** project is still open.

2. Insert a Random Question Slide.

   ❏ on the Filmstrip, select slide **1**

   ❏ choose **Quiz > Random Question Slide**

   A Random Question slide has been added to the Filmstrip between slides **1** and **3**.

3. Link the Random Question Slide to a Question Pool.

   ❏ on the **Quiz Inspector**, (the Quiz Inspector is at the right of the Captivate window, next to the Properties Inspector), select from any of the pools from the **Question Pool** drop-down menu

   ❏ change the **Points** to **1**

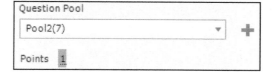

Random Questions Confidence Check

1. Insert four more Random Question Slides.

   Ensure that the Points are set to 1 for each of the slides and that they are linked to any of the Question Pools you like.

   You should now have **five Random Question Slides** in your project.

2. Preview the project and take the quiz. Pay particular attention to the questions that appear.

3. Close the preview.

4. Preview the project and take the quiz again.

   Because you used Random Question Slides that pull questions from three different Pools, the questions you see should be at least a little different than the first time you took the quiz.

5. Close the preview.

6. Save and close the project.

Notes

iCONLOGiC
"Skills and Drills" Learning

Module 5: Accessible eLearning

In This Module You Will Learn About:

And You Will Learn To:

Accessibility and Captivate

You can use Captivate to create eLearning lessons that are accessible to users who have visual, hearing, mobility, or other types of disabilities.

The World Wide Web Consortium (W3C) publishes the Web Content Accessibility Guidelines, a document that specifies what designers should do to their web content to make it accessible. Today, many countries, including the United States, Australia, Canada, Japan, and countries in Europe, have adopted accessibility standards based on those developed by the W3C.

In the United States, the law that governs accessibility is commonly known as Section 508. Part of the Rehabilitation Act of 1973, Section 508 requires that federal agencies, and federally funded organizations, such as colleges and universities, develop or use information technology that is accessible to people with disabilities.

Generally speaking, eLearning is considered accessible if it can be accessed and used by a learner who does not have to rely on a single sense or ability. Learners should be able to move through lessons using only a keyboard *or* a mouse. In addition, your lessons should include visual and auditory elements to support both hearing and visually impaired users.

One of the easiest things you can do to make your Captivate projects accessible is to select Enable Accessibility within an open project (Windows users, **Edit > Preferences > Project > Publish Settings**; Mac users, **Adobe Captivate > Preferences > Project > Publish Settings**). Combining this selection with filling in the Project name and Description (**File > Project Info**) allows an assistive device to read the name and description aloud when a learner accesses the lesson.

The following Captivate elements are accessible when Enable Accessibility is selected:

- ☐ Project name
- ☐ Project description
- ☐ Slide accessibility text
- ☐ Slide names
- ☐ Text buttons
- ☐ Playback controls (The function of each button is read by screen readers.)
- ☐ Password protection (When a Captivate SWF file is password protected, the prompt for a password is read by screen readers.)
- ☐ Question slides (Some Question slides are not considered accessible. Multiple choice and true/false are the easiest ones for a visually impaired learner to navigate.)

For more information on creating and viewing accessible content using Adobe products, visit **http://blogs.adobe.com/accessibility/**. You can learn more about Section 508 by visiting **www.section508.gov**.

Student Activity: Set Document Information

1. Open **ComplyMe** from the Captivate9BeyondData folder.

2. Add Document Information that will be read by a screen reader.

   ☐ choose **File > Project Info**

   The Preferences dialog box appears.

   ☐ in the **Author** field, type **Biff Bifferson**

   ☐ in the **Company** field, type **Super Simplistic Solutions**

   ☐ in the **E-mail** field, type **biff.bifferson@supersimplisticsolutions.com**

   ☐ in the **Website** field, type **www.supersimplisticsolutions.com**

   ☐ in the **Copyright** field, type **2016, Super Simplistic Solutions. All rights reserved.**

   ☐ in the **Project Name** field, type **Creating New Folders: An Interactive Simulation**

   ☐ in the **Description** field, type **This simulation will teach you how to create new folders on your computer.**

Project: Information	
Author:	Biff Bifferson
Company:	Super Simplistic Solutions
E-mail:	biff.bifferson@supersimplisticsolutions.com
Website:	www.supersimplisticsolutions.com
Copyright:	2016, Super Simplistic Solutions. All rights reserved.
Project Name:	Creating New Folders: An Interactive Simulation
Description:	This simulation will teach you how to create new folders on your computer.

   Keep in mind that although you filled in several of the Project Information fields, only the Project Name and Description you typed is useful for compliance. This text is read aloud by an assistive device when the lesson is opened by the learner.

3. Leave the Preferences dialog box open for the next activity.

Student Activity: Enable Accessibility

1. Ensure that the **ComplyMe** project is still open and the **Preferences** dialog box is still open.

2. Enable Accessibility for the project.

   ❏ from the **Project** category, select **Publish Settings**

   ❏ select **Enable Accessibility** to turn the option on

Project: Publish Settings

Frames Per Second: 30

☑ Publish Adobe Connect metadata.

☑ Include Mouse

☑ Enable Accessibility

☐ Restrict keyboard tabbing to slide items only

☐ Hide selection rectangle for slide items in HTML5

☑ Include Audio

☑ Publish Audio as Mono

☑ Play tap audio for recorded typing

Externalize Resources: ☐ Skin

☐ Widgets

☐ FMR SWF

☐ Animations

By selecting Enable Accessibility, you have enabled your published lessons to be viewed by devices, browsers, and assistive software that support accessibility.

Note: Enable Accessibility is on by default in all Captivate projects, and there is little reason to ever disable it. I disabled the feature in this project for training purposes only.

   ❏ click the **OK** button

3. Save your work.

I'd like to be able to tell you adding some Project Information and clicking a check box was all there is to making a project Section 508 compliant. Unfortunately, you have more to do. And although there's much to do, none of what you're about to work through is difficult. It takes time (it could take up to 30% longer to produce an accessible project than a project without accessibility), but nothing about adding accessibility to a Captivate project is difficult.

Accessibility Text

Once you have selected Enable Accessibility, your published Captivate lessons can be read by a screen reader. Screen readers are programs that use auditory feedback to read screen information to a learner. In addition, the screen reader acts as a mouse pointer, providing navigation via keyboard commands.

According to Axistive (**http://www.axistive.com**), "the three main screen readers in North America are (in order of market share) **JAWS**, **Window-Eyes**, and **Hal**, which together sell around 3,000 (units) yearly."

Student Activity: Add Accessibility Text to Slides

1. Ensure that the **ComplyMe** project is still open.

2. Add Slide Accessibility text to a slide.

   ☐ on the **Filmstrip**, double-click slide **1**

   ☐ on the **Properties Inspector**, click the menu in the top right and choose **Accessibility**

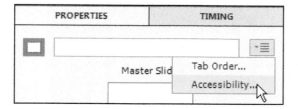

The Slide Accessibility dialog box opens. Screen readers will not "see" slide background images. When a visually impaired learner accesses this slide, the assistive device reads the Slide Accessibility text aloud.

   ☐ type **Welcome to Skills and Drills training. Lesson 1: Creating New Folders. Click the Continue button when you are ready to begin.**

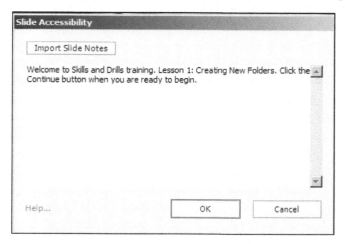

   ☐ click the **OK** button

3. Name a slide.

❏ on the **Properties Inspector**, click within the **Name** field

❏ type **Begin Lesson** and then press [**enter**] on your keyboard

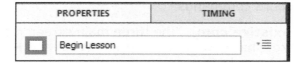

The name appears both in the Name field and beneath the slide on the Filmstrip. This text is also read aloud by assistive devices.

4. Save your work.

Student Activity: Import Slide Audio

1. Ensure that the **ComplyMe** project is still open.

2. Add Audio to slide 1.

   ❑ on the Filmstrip, right-click slide **1** and choose **Audio > Import**

   ❑ navigate to the **Captivate9BeyondData** folder

   ❑ open the **Cp9BeyondAudio** folder and then open **comply_slide1.wav**

   The Slide Audio dialog box opens.

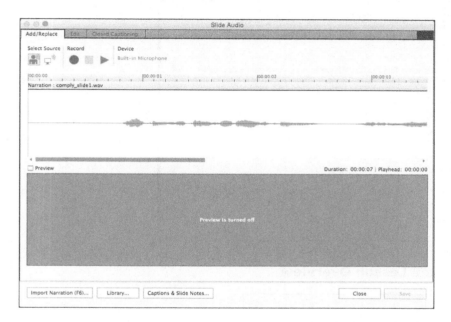

   ❑ click the **Close** button

   Audio is added to the slide (you can confirm this via the speaker icon visible on the slide's Filmstrip thumbnail).

   Are you wondering why you added audio to a slide that already includes Accessibility Text? The audio is for the benefit of learners who are *not* visually disabled. Many people assume that a project is compliant if it includes Accessibility Text *or* slide audio, and if both exist, they will be in direct conflict with each other. In fact, learners who are visually impaired typically rely solely on the screen reader and ignore (or even mute) the slide audio. I've been told by more than one visually impaired learner that the slide audio is annoying, often sounding like the narrator is speaking in slow motion.

Accessibility Text Confidence Check

1. Select slide **2** on the Filmstrip and, from the top right of the **Properties Inspector**, click the menu and choose **Accessibility**.

2. Add the following Accessibility text: **During this interactive lesson you will have a chance to create a new folder. New folders can be created in any window. While you can give a folder any name up to 255 characters, it's a good idea to keep the character count smaller rather than larger.**

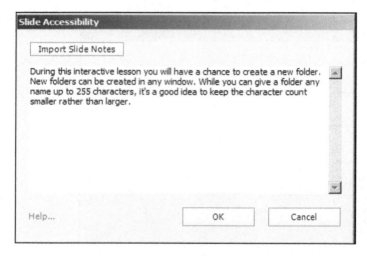

3. Name slide 2 **Lesson Overview**.

4. Add the following audio to slide **2**: **comply_slide2.wav**.

5. When the Audio Import Options dialog box appears, select the first option (to show the slide for that same amount of time as the length of the audio). If you see this dialog box throughout this Confidence Check, always choose the first option.

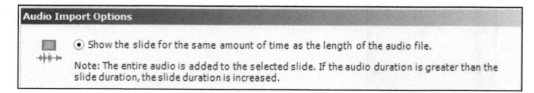

6. Go to slide **3** and add the following Accessibility text to the slide: **To create a new folder, first select the File menu.**

7. Name the slide **Select File menu**.

8. Add the following audio to slide **3**: **comply_slide3.wav**.

9. Go to slide **5** and add the following Accessibility text to the slide: **Now select the New menu item.**

---

10. Name the slide **Select New Command**.

11. Add the following audio to slide **5**: **comply_slide5.wav**.

12. Go to slide **6** and add the following Accessibility text to the slide: **The final step is to select the Folder menu item. Go ahead and do that now.**

13. Name the slide **Select Folder Command**.

14. Add the following audio to slide **6**: **comply_slide6.wav**.

15. Go to slide **8** and add the following Accessibility text to the slide: **And there's your new folder. Go ahead and select the new folder to end this lesson.**

16. Name the slide **Select the New Folder**.

17. Add the following audio to slide **8**: **comply_slide8.wav**.

18. Preview the project.

    There should be audio on the appropriate slides. However, none of the buttons on the slides are *keyboard accessible.* Learners should be able to press a key on the keyboard to move from slide to slide. You will fix this problem next.

19. Close the preview.

20. Save and close the project.

Shortcut Keys

You can attach a keyboard shortcut to any interactive object in Captivate (interactive objects include buttons, click boxes, text entry boxes, and rollover slidelets). Not only are shortcut keys an important component of accessibility, but many users will consider your lessons to be easier to navigate. In fact, many users who might be fully capable of using a mouse to click objects elect to instead use shortcut keys as an alternative to using the mouse.

> **Note:** Although you can use just about any keyboard shortcut or combination of keys as your shortcut keys, you should carefully test those shortcuts in several web browsers. Some keyboard shortcuts are reserved by the browser. The keys might work as expected when you preview the lesson from within Captivate. However, when you preview the lesson in a browser, the keys might be intercepted by the web browser and not work as expected. (For instance, the [**F1**] key historically displays the browser's Help window.)

Student Activity: Add Shortcut Keys

1. Open **Shortcut_CCMe** from the Captivate9BeyondData folder.

2. Attach a shortcut key to a button.

   ❏ on slide **1**, double-click the **Continue** button

   ❏ on the **Properties Inspector**, select the **Actions** tab

   ❏ just beneath **Shortcut**, click the radio button

   ❏ on your keyboard, press [**enter**] (PC) or [**return**] (Mac)

   The shortcut appears in the Shortcut field.

3. Attach a shortcut key to the button on slide 2.

   ❏ go to slide **2**

   ❏ select the **Continue** button

   ❏ on the **Properties Inspector**, select the **Actions** tab

   ❏ just beneath **Shortcut**, click the radio button

   ❏ on your keyboard, press [**enter**] (PC) or [**return**] (Mac)

4. Attach a multikey shortcut to a click box.

  ❏ go to slide **3**

  ❏ on the **Timeline**, select the **Click Box**

  ❏ on the **Properties Inspector**, select the **Actions** tab

  ❏ just beneath **Shortcut**, click the radio button

  ❏ on your keyboard, press [**alt**] [**f**] (Mac users, press [**option**] [**f**])

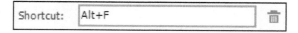

Note: If you're a Windows user, pressing [**alt**] [**f**] likely opens Captivate's File menu. This action does no harm, and you can simply close the menu.

5. Test the shortcut keys.

  ❏ select slide **1**

  ❏ choose **Preview > Next 5 Slides**

  ❏ when the first slide appears, press [**enter**] or [**return**] to go to the next slide

  ❏ when the second slide appears, press [**enter**] or [**return**] to go to the next slide

  ❏ Windows users, when the third slide appears, press [**alt**] [**f**] ([**option**] [**f**] on a Mac) to go to the next slide

The keys should have worked as expected. Let's see what happens when you preview the lesson through a web browser.

6. Close the preview.

7. Preview via a web browser.

  ❏ choose **Preview > In Browser**

  ❏ after the lesson begins, press [**enter**] or [**return**] to move through the first two slides

  ❏ when the third slide appears, press [**alt**] [**f**] ([**option**] [**f**] on a Mac) to go to the next slide

Ooops! If you are using a Windows-based browser, the [**alt**] [**f**] combination probably worked, and you advanced to the next slide. (I noticed that the combination did not work in Windows Edge.) However, the [**alt**] [**f**] combination also opened the File menu in the browser. If you are a Mac user running Safari, the [**option**] [**f**] combination isn't supported. Because you cannot stop keys from activating web browser functions or always predict how

some key combinations work in every web browser, it's best to shy away from key combinations and use single-key shortcuts instead.

8. Close the browser window and return to the Captivate project.

9. Edit assigned shortcut keys.

    ☐ go to slide **3**

    ☐ on the Timeline, select the Click Box

    ☐ on the **Properties Inspector**, click in the Shortcut field and press [**f**] on your keyboard

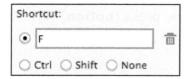

10. Preview the project **In Browser** and ensure that the shortcut keys work as expected.

11. Close the browser window and return to the Captivate project.

Keyboard Shortcut Confidence Check

1. Still working in the **Shortcut_CCMe** project, go to slide **5** and attach the following letter shortcut to the click box: **N**.

2. Go to slide **6** and attach the following letter shortcut to the click box: **F**.

3. Go to slide **8** and attach the following letter shortcut to the click box: **F**.

4. Preview the project **In Browser** and ensure that the shortcut keys work as expected.

5. When finished, close the browser window and return to the Captivate project.

6. On slide **1**, open the Slide Accessibility text dialog box (you learned how on page 75).

7. Add the following text after the word "button": **(or press ENTER on your keyboard)**.

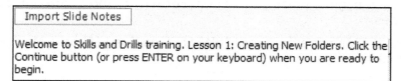

8. Continue through the rest of the slides, adding Accessibility Text as necessary so that screen readers alert a learner as to which shortcut key to press when a slide with interactivity is accessed.

9. When finished, save your work.

Closed Captioning

Closed captioning (CC) allows you to provide descriptive information that explains the audio recording in written text. If your playbar contains a CC button (most playbars do by default), a learner has the option to click the CC button, which displays a panel where the closed caption text appears.

Student Activity: Add Closed Captions

1. Ensure that the **Shortcut_CCMe** project is still open.

2. Show the Advanced Audio Management dialog box.

   ☐ choose **Audio > Audio Management**

   Six of the slides contain audio clips. (Notice that the Sound column for those slides contains the word "Yes.") You can add Closed Captions only to slides containing slide-level audio.

3. Add Closed Captions to a slide.

   ☐ from the **Slide/Object** column, select **Begin Lesson**

   ☐ at the bottom of the dialog box, click the **Closed Caption** tool

The Slide Audio dialog box opens, and the Closed Captioning tab is selected. You can add closed captions anywhere on the waveform. To begin, you'll be adding a closed caption at the beginning. But first, let's zoom away from the waveform a bit so you can see more of it.

   ☐ drag the zoom slider **left** to around **20**

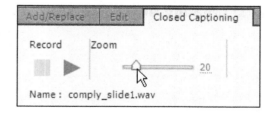

   ☐ click in front of the first segment on the waveform

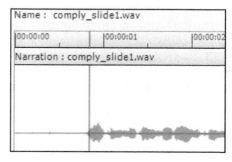

❏ click the **Add Closed Caption** tool

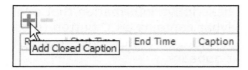

❏ in the Caption area, type **Welcome to skills and drills training.**

The caption text appears in Row 1, and there is an orange caption mark and the number "1" on the waveform.

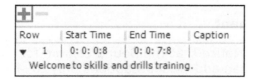

4. Add a second Closed Caption to the slide.

   ❏ on the waveform, click in front of the second segment (just before the 3 second mark)

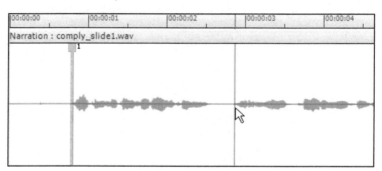

   ❏ click the **Add Closed Caption** tool
   ❏ in the Caption area, type **Lesson 1: Creating New Folders.**

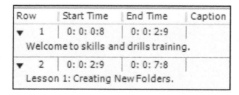

5. Add a third Closed Caption to the slide.

   ❏ on the waveform, click in front of the third segment (just before the 5.5 second mark)

   ❏ click the **Add Closed Caption** tool

   ❏ in the Caption area, type **Click the Continue button when you are ready to begin.**

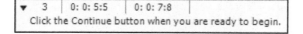

Your three closed captions should look similar to this:

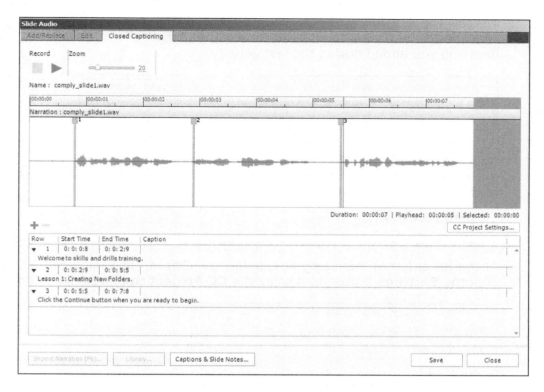

❏ click the **Save** button

❏ click the **Close** button

❏ click the **OK** button to close the Advanced Audio Management dialog box

6. Save your work.

Adobe Captivate 9: Beyond The Essentials

Closed Captions Confidence Check

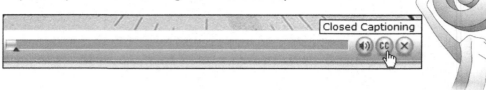

1. Preview the first five slides. As soon as slide **1** appears, click the **CC** button on the playbar to see the Closed Captions you added during the last activity.

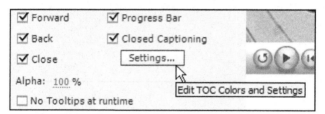

   Notice that the Closed Captions are synchronized to match the audio, word-for-word. However, the Closed Caption text is a bit hard to read. You will fix that next.

2. Close the preview.

3. Show the Skin Editor (**Project > Skin Editor**).

4. At the lower left of the dialog box, below the Closed Captioning check box, click the **Settings** button to display the **CC Project Settings** dialog box.

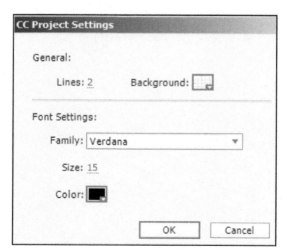

5. From the General area, change the Lines to **2** (this lowers the height of the Closed Caption area).

6. From the Font Settings area, change the Family to **Verdana** and the Size to **15**.

7. Click the **OK** button.

8. Close the Skin Editor window.

© 2015, IconLogic, Inc. All Rights Reserved.

9. Preview the first five slides of the project again. As soon as slide **1** appears, click the CC on the playback controls to see that Verdana is the font used within the Closed Captions.

10. Close the preview.

11. Show the **Audio Management** dialog box (Audio menu).

12. Select the audio for slide **2** (Lesson Overview).

13. Click the Closed Caption tool.

14. Add three Closed Captions in front of the main segments along the waveform. (Consider listening to the audio by clicking the Play button prior to adding the Closed Captions. Doing so helps you position the Closed Captions correctly.)

    During this interactive lesson you will have a chance to create a new folder.

    New folders can be created in any window.

    While you can give a folder any name up to 255 characters, it's a good idea to keep the character count smaller rather than larger.

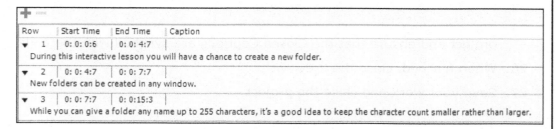

Row	Start Time	End Time	Caption
1	0: 0: 0:6	0: 0: 4:7	During this interactive lesson you will have a chance to create a new folder.
2	0: 0: 4:7	0: 0: 7:7	New folders can be created in any window.
3	0: 0: 7:7	0: 0:15:3	While you can give a folder any name up to 255 characters, it's a good idea to keep the character count smaller rather than larger.

15. Preview the project from slide **1** and review the Closed Captions.

16. When finished, close the preview and save your work.

    As you've probably guessed, Closed Captions aren't difficult to add to your project but can add a significant amount of labor to your production load. Here's a little nugget that might speed things along:

17. Go to slide **3**.

18. Choose **Window > Slide Notes** to open the Slide Notes panel.

19. Click in the Slide Notes panel at the bottom of your window where it says **Click to add notes for the selected slide**.

20. Type: **To create a new folder, first select the File menu.**

21. At the top of the Slide Notes panel, select the Audio CC check box.

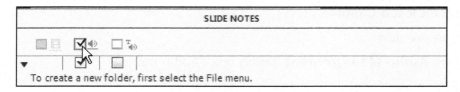

22. Click the **Closed Captioning** button.

23. On the Closed Captioning tab, notice that the Closed Caption has already been added to the waveform. You can drag the closed caption mark to the right to better synchronize the Closed Caption with the audio.

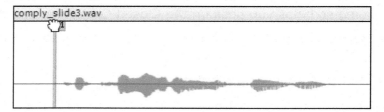

24. Proceed through the rest of the project and add Closed Captions as necessary.

25. When finished adding the Closed Captions to the project, preview the entire project and ensure that the Closed Captions are synched with the audio.

26. When finished, close the Preview.

27. Save your work and close the project.

Tab Order

Learners have always been able to select screen objects on published Captivate lessons by either clicking the mouse or using the [**tab**] key on the keyboard. However, your ability to control which screen objects came into focus when the learner pressed the [**tab**] key *was* beyond your control. I emphasize the word *was*... thanks to Captivate's Tab Order controls, you can now determine which interactive screen objects come into focus when the learner presses the [**tab**] key. As a bonus, the Tab Order you establish also controls when the Accessibility text added to interactive objects is read aloud by a screen reader.

Student Activity: Set a Tab Order

1. Open **TabOrderMe** from the Captivate9BeyondData folder.

   This is a simple, single-slide project containing three interactive buttons. The buttons have been set up to play a sound when clicked.

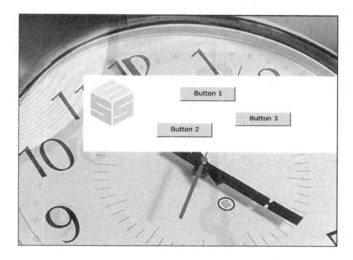

2. Preview the project.

3. Press the [**tab**] key on your keyboard.

   As you press the [**tab**] key, notice that you move around the slide and select each button in a logical order (Button 1, Button 2, and Button 3). After tabbing past Button 3, you are taken around the tools on the playbar and then back to Button 1.

   When learners press the [**tab**] key, you want to forgo logical navigation and have Button 2 be the first button selected, then Button 3, and finally Button 1. You'll set that up next using Captivate's Tab Order feature.

4. Close the Preview.

5. Set a Tab Order.

   ❑ ensure that no slide objects are selected (the Tab Order option isn't available if even one slide object is selected)

❑ on the Properties Inspector, click the menu and choose **Tab Order**

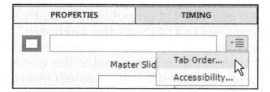

The Tab Order dialog box opens. You will use this dialog box to control the accessibility order of the buttons on the slide. You'll select a button and use the **Move Selected Row Up** arrow to move it into a desired position.

❑ in the **Tab Order** dialog box, select **Second_Button**

❑ click the **Move Selected Row Up** arrow

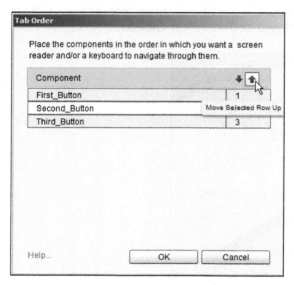

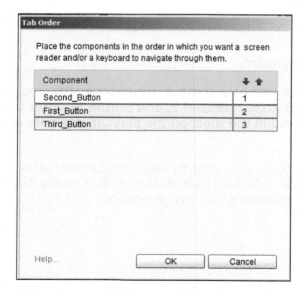

❑ click the **OK** button

Tab Order Confidence Check

1. Open the Tab Order dialog box again.

2. Change the Tab Order so that the Component list matches the image below.

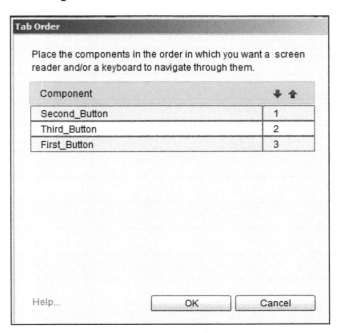

3. Preview the project and press the [**tab**] key on your keyboard to navigate around the slide.

   As you press the [**tab**] key, you should select Button 2 first, Button 3 second, and Button 1 third.

4. Close the preview.

5. Save your work and close the project.

Notes

iCONLOGiC

"Skills and Drills" Learning

Module 6: Variables and Widgets

In This Module You Will Learn About:

And You Will Learn To:

Variables

Variables serve as placeholders for data. The data can be used to provide feedback to the learner, create Actions you will learn to work with Actions on page 129), add content, or configure widgets (you will learn to work with widgets on page 104).

There are two types of variables available in Adobe Captivate: **System** and **User-Defined**. System variables are available in all Captivate projects. System variables include **Movie Information** (such as the current slide and frame), **Movie Metadata** (information about the project such as its name, author, and company), **System Information** (data that can be grabbed from your computer, such as current date and time), and **Quizzing** (lists that allow you to capture quiz data, such as the number of quiz attempts or the percentage of questions answered correctly). User-Defined variables are typically created by you on an as-needed basis. Here's one use case for them. Wouldn't it be great if the learner saw their name throughout a lesson, almost as if you had personalized it just for them? No problem. Create a variable to store the learner's name after they type it. The stored name can be displayed to the learner over and over again. Sound awesome? You'll actually implement that scenario later in this module.

Student Activity: Add Project Information

1. Open **VariableWidgetMe** from the Captivate9BeyondData folder.

2. Add information to the document.

   ❏ choose **File > Project Info**

   The Project Information dialog box opens.

   ❏ in the **Author** field, type **Biff Bifferson**
   ❏ in the **Company** field, type **Super Simplistic Solutions**
   ❏ in the **E-mail** field, type **biff.bifferson@supersimplisticsolutions.com**
   ❏ in the **Website** field, type **www.supersimplisticsolutions.com**
   ❏ in the **Copyright** field, type **2016, Super Simplistic Solutions. All rights reserved.**
   ❏ in the **Project Name** field, type **Working with Variables and Widgets**
   ❏ in the **Description** field, type **This lesson will help you learn how to add variables and widgets to a Captivate project.**

Project: Information

Author: Biff Bifferson
Company: Super Simplistic Solutions
E-mail: biff.bifferson@supersimplisticsolutions.com
Website: www.supersimplisticsolutions.com
Copyright: 2016, Super Simplistic Solutions. All rights reserved.
Project Name: Working with Variables and Widgets
Description: This lesson will help you learn how to add variables and widgets to a Captivate project.

   ❏ click the **OK** button

Student Activity: Insert a System Variable

1. Ensure that the **VariableWidgetMe** project is still open.

2. Insert a text caption.

   ☐ go to slide **1** and choose **Text > Text Caption**
   ☐ type **Welcome to** followed by [**spacebar**]

3. Insert a system variable into the text caption.

   ☐ ensure your insertion point is blinking within the text caption (you cannot insert a variable in a caption without the insertion point)

   ☐ on the **Properties Inspector**, from the **Character** area, click **Insert Variable**

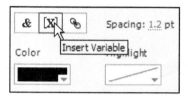

The Insert Variable dialog box opens.

   ☐ from the **Variable Type** drop-down menu, choose **System**
   ☐ from the **View By** drop-down menu, choose **Movie Metadata**

The Movie Metadata is a group of System variables that specifically look into the Project Information dialog box that you just filled out.

   ☐ from the **Variables** drop-down menu, choose **cpInfoProjectName**
   ☐ change the Maximum length to **15**

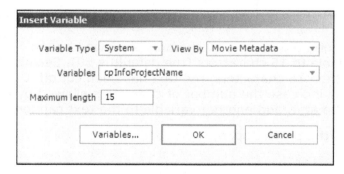

   ☐ click the **OK** button

The variable appears within the text caption.

Variable Preview Confidence Check

1. Drag the text caption and resize it until its size and position look similar to the picture below

2. Save your work.

3. Preview the project.

   Notice two things as the first slide appears. First, the variable gibberish you saw prior to previewing the project has been replaced by the data you typed in the Project Name field back on page 94. *That's cool!* However, the entire name of the project, "Working with Variables and Widgets," isn't showing up.

   > Welcome to Working with Va

   A moment ago you changed the number of characters allowed by the cpInfoProjectName variable to 15 characters (the default is 50). Because the project name is longer than 15 characters, the text has been cut off. During the next activity, you will increase the number of characters allowed by the variable and, while you're at it, add another variable to the text caption.

4. Close the preview (keep the project open).

Student Activity: Edit a System Variable

1. Ensure that the **VariableWidgetMe** project is still open.

2. Edit the maximum number of characters displayed by a variable.

   ☐ on slide **1**, select and delete the variable text **$$cpInfoProjectName$$** from the Text Caption

   ☐ on the **Properties Inspector**, **Character** area, click **Insert Variable**

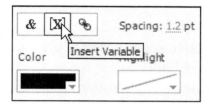

The Insert Variable dialog box reopens.

   ☐ from the **Variable Type** drop-down menu, ensure that **System** is selected

   ☐ from the **View By** drop-down menu, select **Movie Metadata**

   ☐ from the **Variables** drop-down menu, select **cpInfoProjectName**

   ☐ change the **Maximum length** to **25**

Variables	cpInfoProjectName ▾
Maximum length	25

   ☐ click the **OK** button

Before previewing the project and seeing if the Maximum length field has changed things for the better, notice that the text caption resized after you inserted the updated variable. To prevent objects from resizing after you make edits, display the **Preferences** dialog box, select the first **Defaults**, and from the **General** area, deselect **Autosize Captions**.

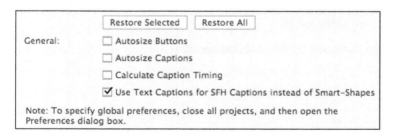

I never allow Captivate to Autosize anything or to calculate the timing for my captions. I find that all three options make more work for me in the long run. For instance, let's say that I leave the options selected. I then spend time sizing a caption to a specific size and setting a specific play time for the caption. If I later make even a simple change to the text within the caption (change the font size, for instance), both the caption's size *and* timing are reset by Captivate. *More work for me? No thanks!*

System Variables Confidence Check

1. Resize the text caption larger (it needs to be big enough to display a few sentences).

2. Preview the project.

   Increasing the maximum length has improved things, to a point. However, the entire project name still doesn't appear. You'll have to make another change to the Maximum length field of the variable.

3. Close the preview and save your work.

4. Still working on slide **1** of the VariableWidgetMe project, delete the variable text **$$cpInfoProjectName$$** in the text caption.

5. Insert the **cpInfoProjectName** variable again. However, this time change the Maximum length to **50**.

6. Preview the project and confirm that the entire project name appears in the text caption.

7. Close the preview and then save your work.

8. Double-click the text caption on slide **1**, click after the **$$cpInfoProjectName$$**, and type a period to complete the sentence.

9. Press [**enter**] a few times to add some white space.

10. Type **This presentation has been developed by** and press [**spacebar**].

11. Resize the text caption larger and then insert the **cpInfoAuthor** variable (the variable is grouped with the Movie Metadata variables) with a Maximum length of **50**.

12. Type **of** after the **$$cpInfoAuthor$$** text.

13. Insert the **cpInfoCompany** variable with a Maximum length of **50**.

14. Type a period at the end of the text.

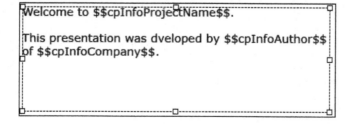

15. Preview the project. If the text does not appear in the text caption, you will most likely need to close the preview and resize the text caption. (If you are sure that the text caption is large enough, you may need to replace the variable text that is not appearing with a variable with a larger Maximum length.)

16. Close the preview and then save your work.

User Variables

During the next few activities, you're going to create a variable that gathers information typed by the learner. Using this technique, you'll be able to customize the eLearning lesson for each learner. To begin, you will create a user variable named learner_name. You'll attach the learner_name variable to a Text Entry Box on slide 2. When the learner enters his/her name into the Text Entry Box, the typed name is stored in memory (thanks to the learner_name variable). You'll next insert the learner_name variable within a text caption on slide 3. Because the learner_name variable is attached to the text entry box on the previous slide, the name the learner types is displayed within the text caption.

Student Activity: Create a User Variable

1. Ensure that the **VariableWidgetMe** project is still open.

2. Create a user variable.

   ☐ choose **Project > Variables**

   The Variables dialog box opens. You use this dialog box to create, edit, and update variables.

   ☐ from the **Type** drop-down menu, choose **User** (if necessary)

   ☐ click the **Add New** button at the right of the dialog box and, in the **Name** field, type **learner_name**

   When naming a new variable, you can use any of the following formats: LearnerName, learner_name, learnerName. The format you choose is up to you, but you should be consistent, and you should not use spaces.

   ☐ in the Value field, type **Learner**

   Although it is not a requirement to add a Value to every variable, it's a good idea to do so. By using a value of Learner for this variable, you are telling Captivate to display the name Learner if the learner does not type a name into the lesson as instructed.

   ☐ in the Description field type **This variable will gather the name of the learner so that it can be used throughout the lesson.**

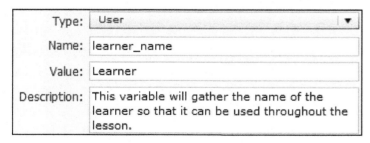

   As with the Value field, a variable does not require a Description. However, including a Description saves you time and heartache down the road if you forget what the variable was supposed to do.

   ☐ click the **Save** button

The new variable appears at the bottom of the Variables dialog box.

❑ click the **Close** button

3. Save your work.

Student Activity: Use a Variable to Gather Learner Data

1. Ensure that the **VariableWidgetMe** project is still open.

2. Add learner instructions on slide 2.

   ☐ go to slide **2**

   ☐ choose **Text > Text Caption**

   ☐ add the following text to the text caption: **Before we begin, let's learn a little more about you. Please type your first name into the space below. When you are done, press ENTER or click the Continue button.**

3. Resize and position the text caption until your slide looks similar to the picture below

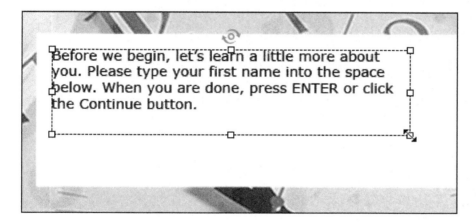

4. Save your work.

5. Insert a Text Entry Box.

   ☐ still working on slide 2, choose **Text > Text Entry Box**

   A small Text Entry Box has been added to the slide, along with a Submit button and a Hint caption. You will be editing the text on the button and removing the Hint caption soon.

6. Associate a user variable with the Text Entry Box.

   ☐ ensure that the **Text Entry Box** is selected

   ☐ on the **Properties Inspector**, **Style** tab, click the **Variable** drop-down menu and choose **learner_name**

Now that the variable and the text entry box are associated, when a learner types anything in the text entry box, the information is retained by the learner_name variable until the lesson is closed. The retained data can be displayed within Text Captions throughout the lesson. You will learn how to do that soon.

7. Set the Action for the Text Entry Box.

    ❒ on the **Properties Inspector**, select the **Actions** tab

    ❒ from **On Success** drop-down menu, choose **Go to the next slide**

    ❒ from the **Attempts** area, ensure **Infinite** is selected

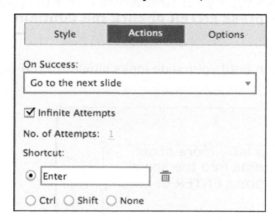

8. Remove the Hint caption.

    ❒ from the **Display** area, deselect **Hint**

User-Defined Variables Confidence Check

1. Resize and reposition the Text Entry Box and Submit button until your slide looks similar to the picture below.

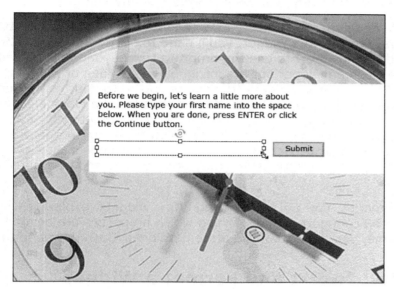

2. Go to slide **3** and insert the **learner_name** User variable into the text caption as shown in the picture below (when inserting the Variable, set the Maximum length to **100**).

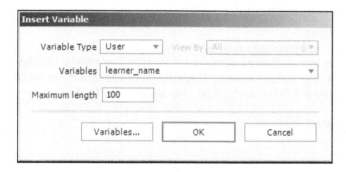

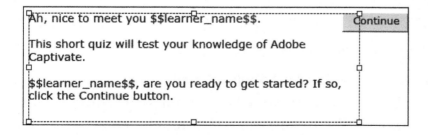

3. Preview the project. When you get to slide **2**, type your first name as instructed, and when you get to slide **3**... wait for it... MAGIC! The name you typed on slide **2** has been collected and appears on slide **3**.

4. Close the preview and then save your work.

Widgets

If you are an Adobe Flash developer, you can create objects that can, to a limited extent, be configured in Captivate. As a Flash developer, you would publish these files from Flash as SWFs. In Captivate, those SWFs (known as widgets because they can usually be modified in some way) can be imported like any animation.

Widgets give Captivate developers the ability to extend Captivate's functionality without limits. Of course, to create a widget, you'll need to own Adobe Flash CS3 or newer, and you'll need to know how to use the program (far beyond the basic skill level). If you are not a Flash developer but are intrigued by the idea of widgets, all is not lost. Captivate includes several widgets (they were copied to your computer during the Captivate installation process). You do not have to be a Flash developer, nor do you need to have Flash on your computer to insert widgets into your Captivate project. There are basically three types of widgets: **Static** (they are not interactive and only display information), **Interactive** (they change their appearance or function based on user input), and **Question** (they allow you to add new question types to your project).

During the next few activities, you will be inserting a few widgets, exploring which parts of the widget can be configured, and learning which properties are beyond your control (unless, of course, you are one of the aforementioned Flash developers).

Student Activity: Insert and Format a Widget

1. Ensure that the **VariableWidgetMe** project is still open.

2. Insert the emailIcon widget.

   ☐ go to the last slide of the project (slide **10**)

   ☐ choose **Insert > Widget**

   The Open dialog box appears and you should be in the Captivate **Widgets** folder. If not, navigate to the folder where Captivate is installed on your computer. Open the **Gallery** folder and then the **Widgets** folder.

   ☐ open the **emailIcon.swf** widget

   The Widget Properties dialog box opens.

   ☐ in the **Label** field, change the **Label** to **Email**

   ☐ in the To field, type **biff.bifferson@supersimplisticsolutions.com**

   ☐ in the Subject line, type **I'd like more information about your products and services.**

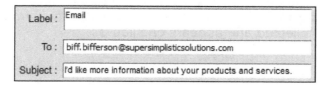

❏ change the Family to **Verdana**

❏ ensure that the Style is **Regular**

❏ change the Size to **13**

❏ click the **OK** button

3. Save your work.

Widget Confidence Check

1. Drag the widget until its slide position is similar to the image below

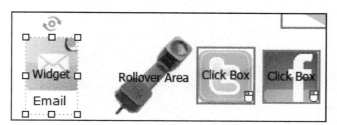

2. With the widget selected, use the Timing Inspector to change the widget's Display Timing to **Rest of Slide**.

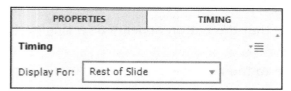

3. Preview the project. When you get to the last slide, click the Email icon.

   Your email program should start. Notice that the email is already addressed and that the subject line is filled in.

4. Close the email without sending or saving it.

5. Return to Captivate and close the preview.

6. Save and close the project.

7. Open **PerpetuateMe** from the **Captivate9BeyondData** folder.

8. On slide **1**, insert the **PerpetualButton_AS3** widget. (Review the instruction that appears and then click the **OK** button.)

9. On the Timing Inspector, change the Timing for the widget to Display For time to **Rest of Project**.

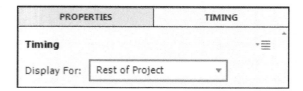

10. Still on slide **1**, move the **PerpetualButtons** widget to the lower right of the slide as shown in the picture below.

Now for the coolness of Perpetual buttons...

11. Preview the project.

    As the first slide fades in, notice that the button appears as a single, right-facing button.

12. Click the button on slide **1** to go to the next slide.

    Hopefully, you'll appreciate that Perpetual buttons include a Go to next slide action that automatically moves you through the presentation (but that's not the coolest part of Perpetual buttons).

13. Keep moving through the presentation. As you move through the slide show, notice that the appearance of the button stays consistent until you reach the last slide. At that point, the button changes appearance automatically and now becomes a single, left-facing button. *Cool! Cool! Cool!*

    The trick to getting the Perpetual button to work? I'm not going to lie to you and say you could make your own button (widget) in a snap. In reality, you'd need experience with Adobe Flash. However, importing the widget and displaying it for the entire project (as you did during step 9 above) is what makes the widget work for the entire project.

14. Close the preview.

15. Save and close the project.

Module 7: Interactions

In This Module You Will Learn About:

- Learning Interactions, page 108
- Drag and Drop, page 112
- Multi-State Objects, page 123

And You Will Learn To:

- Insert a Process Circle, page 108
- Explore a Drag and Drop Project, page 112
- Create a Drag and Drop Interaction, page 116
- Change Object States, page 123

Learning Interactions

Interactions, also referred to as Smart Learning Interactions, are powerful widgets that allow you to quickly insert interactive objects onto a slide. Captivate ships with a wide range of Interactions, such as Process Cycles and Pyramids, and you can download others. As you work with Interactions, you'll find that you can customize not only the content but also the look and feel of the Interaction.

Student Activity: Insert a Process Circle

1. Open **InteractMe** from the Captivate9BeyondData folder.

2. Insert an Interaction.

   ☐ on the Filmstrip, select slide **2**

   ☐ on the toolbar, click **Interactions** and choose **Learning Interactions**

The Select Interaction dialog box opens.

☐ select **Process Circle**

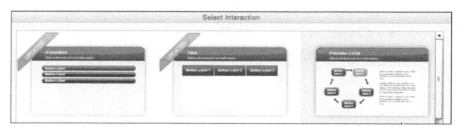

☐ click the **Insert** button

The **Configure interaction** dialog box opens.

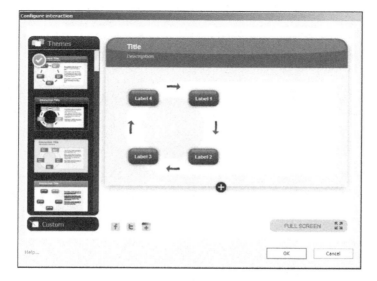

3. Select a Theme.

    ☐ with the Configure Interactions dialog box still open, scroll down the list of **Themes** and select **Theme 15 Green**

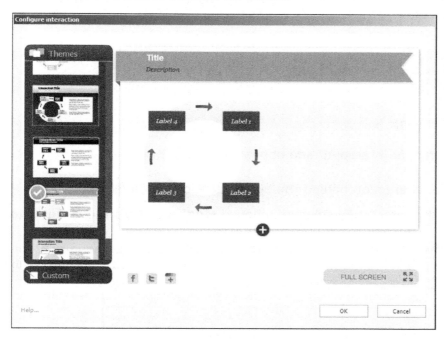

4. Add a Title and Description.

    ☐ double-click the word **Title** and select it and replace it with:
    Top Chocolate Bars

    Note: When attempting to select Learning Interactions text, you might find that it takes more than a few clicks to select text. I've seen it take six, seven, even eight clicks to highlight text (sometimes just two). I don't know why there is such "click inconsistency" in this area of Captivate, but know that it's not you... and keep on clicking.

    ☐ select the word **Description** and replace it with: **Based on international sales.**

5. Add Label text.

    ☐ select **Label 1** to make it the active label

    ☐ select the phrase **Label 1** and replace it with your favorite chocolate bar

6. Add Button Content.

❏ just to the right of the label you just edited, select the **Button Content 1**

❏ replace the text with a description of the chocolate bar you typed into the label field

❏ click the **OK** button

The Interaction is created and appears on slide **2**.

7. Send the Interaction behind the button already on the slide.

❏ with the Interaction selected, choose **Modify > Arrange > Send to Back**

8. Resize the interaction so it fits on the slide (if you resize the interaction while pressing [**shift**] on your keyboard, you'll be able to resize proportionally).

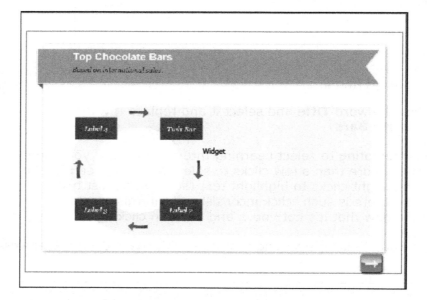

9. Test the Interaction.

❏ choose **Preview > Project**

When you get to slide 2, click the candy bar label you added and its description appears. When you click the other labels, they'll spin into view. How awesome is that?

10. Close the Preview.

Interactions Confidence Check

1. Double-click the Interaction to reopen the Widget Properties dialog box.

2. Replace the remaining labels with your favorite candy bars and descriptions.

3. Preview the Project and test the Interaction.

4. Close the preview.

5. Save and close the project.

Drag and Drop

It's likely that you have heard the saying "you are limited only by your imagination." Often times that saying is just lip service... a vendor trying to sell you a product. However, the ability to add Drag and Drop functionality to your eLearning project does the saying proud... and it's free. Using Captivate's Drag and Drop Interaction, you can engage your learner at a very high level (and with no programming skills).

During the lessons that follow you will add the Drag and Drop functionality necessary to complete a soft skills lesson on appropriate work attire.

Student Activity: Explore a Drag and Drop Project

1. Open **DragDropMeDone** from the Captivate9BeyondData folder.

2. Preview the project.

   At the left, say hello to James. At the right, notice the clothes. Your mission, should you choose to accept it, is to ensure that James is dressed appropriately for work.

3. Test the interaction.

   ❏ drag the **beer tee** to James' feet

   Since the shirt is not intended to serve as shoes, the shirt automatically returns to its original position.

   ❏ drag the **beer tee** to James' tee-shirt

   Since the beer tee can be worn in this part of James' body, the shirt snaps into position.

   ❏ drag either the **cut-off shorts** or the **slacks** to the appropriate area on James

   ❏ drag either the **oxfords** or the **sandals** to the appropriate area on James

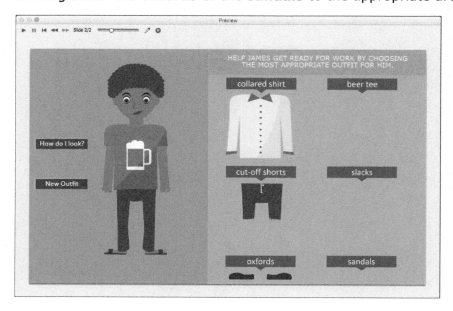

❏ at the left, click the **How do I look** button

Because this particular ensemble isn't quite appropriate for work, you're prompted to try again. Not only that, but did you notice that the expression on James' face changed? That's a "state" in action, something you'll cover after tackling Drag and Drop.

❏ at the left, click the **New Outfit** button

The slide is reset.

❏ drag the **collared shirt**, **slacks**, and **oxfords** to the appropriate area on James

❏ click the **How do I look** button

Because you have positioned the clothes correctly, the "I look sharp" caption appears. In addition, the expression on James' face reflects just how ready for work he is!

4. Close the preview.

5. Explore the drop zones.

   ❐ go to slide **2**

On James, notice that there are three smart shapes positioned strategically on his body. These shapes serve as drop zones for the clothing. Each of the shapes has been formatted with 0% opacity so they are see-through.

In the activities that follow, you'll build the interaction by targeting the three drop zones with specific items of clothing.

6. Explore the Drag and Drop Inspector.

   ☐ on the slide, select the **top drop zone** by clicking on James' chest

   ☐ at the right of the Captivate window, select the **Drag and Drop** inspector

   Note: If the Drag and Drop inspector isn't on your screen (it usually appears automatically), choose **Window > Drag and Drop**.

   There are several options on the **Drag and Drop** inspector that allow you to precisely control the drag and drop functionality. You'll be playing with some of these options soon.

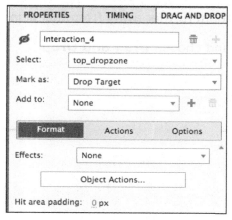
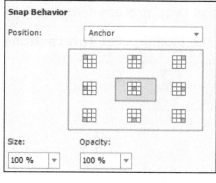
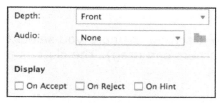

7. Close the project (there is no need to save it).

Student Activity: Create a Drag and Drop Interaction

1. Open **DragDropMeStart** from the Captivate9BeyondData folder.

2. Insert a Drag and Drop Interaction.

   ☐ select slide **2**

   ☐ change the **View Magnification** enough that you can see the entire slide (including all of the clothes at the right)

   Note: Zoom as far away from the slide as practical. During the next step, if you're too close to select slide objects you'll have to cancel the Drag and Drop process if you want to zoom further away from the slide.

   ☐ on the toolbar, click **Interactions** and choose **Drag and Drop**

   The Drag and Drop wizard opens. This first screen is where you select the **Drag Sources** (the slide objects that learners can drag). The clothes are going to be the sources.

   ☐ on the slide, select **all six** of the clothing items (using the [**shift**]-click technique works great for selecting multiple objects)

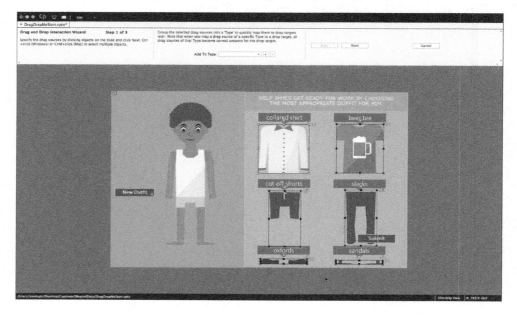

   ☐ click the **Next** button

The second screen allows you to specify the **Drop Targets**. In this case, the targets are the three smart shapes covering James.

❒ on the slide, select **all three smart shapes** covering James' body

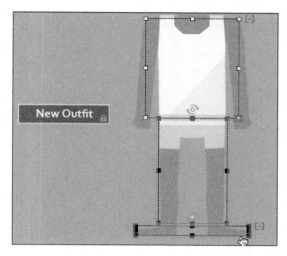

❒ click the **Next** button

The third and final screen allows you to associate **Drag Sources** with **Drop Targets**.

❒ on the slide, drag the **+ sign** in the middle of the **collared shirt** to the **top Drop Target**

❒ on the slide, drag the **+ sign** in the middle of the **slacks** to the **middle Drop Target**

❒ on the slide, drag the **+ sign** in the middle of the **oxfords** to the **bottom Drop Target**

❒ click the **Finish** button

Drag and Drop Confidence Check

1. Move the Submit button to the left of James and change the button caption to **How do I look?**

On the slide, there are two feedback captions (a green Success Smart Shape and, behind that, a Failure Smart Shape).

2. Drag the Success Caption out of the way.

3. Move the Failure Caption (the purple one) to the left of James' head.

4. Change its text to **That's not it. Click New Outfit to try again**.

---

5. Drag the **Success Caption** to the left of James' head.

6. Replace the Smart Shape with a **Cloud Callout Smart Shape** (right-click the caption, choose **Replace Smart Shape**, and then choose **Cloud Callout**).

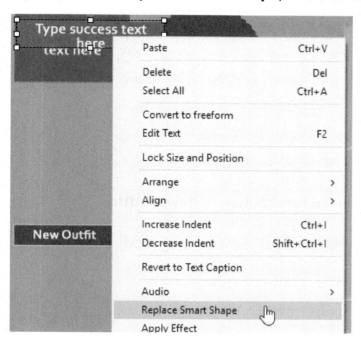

7. Change the text in the Smart Shape to **I look sharp!**

8. Drag the tail of the smart shape so it points to James' head.

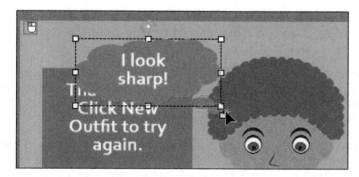

9. Insert a **Reset** button by selecting **Reset** on the Drag and Drop Inspector, **Actions** tab.

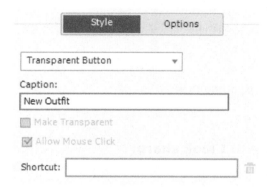

10. Change the caption on the Reset button to **New Outfit**.

11. On the slide, position and resize the **New Outfit** button over the original **New Outfit** button.

Are you wondering why you added two New Outfit buttons to the slide? Like a quiz question, you can set a Drag and Drop interaction to have a single, many, or infinite attempts. If set to a single attempt, the submit and reset buttons will disappear after the learner attempts the Drag and Drop.

If the learner wants to try again, you need a way to reset the scene. That is accomplished here by jumping back one slide via a button under the reset button. The button looks like the reset button (New Outfit) so to the learner, it appears to be the same button. When the learner clicks the regular button, they are simply taken back one slide so that when we enter the second slide, the Drag and Drop can be attempted again.

You might be thinking, why not just set the number of attempt to infinite and be done with it? That's a great idea, but in that case the Failure state (where James frowns) will never occur because when you allow infinite attempts, the learner can never fail. To provide a scenario where a Failure action occurs, but the learner can do the activity again, you have set the number of attempts to one and provide the "extra" button that basically resets the activity.

Next you need to ensure that clothing items do not end up on the wrong part of James' body. You'll accomplish the task via the Object Actions button on the Drag and Drop Inspector.

12. Select the **top_dropzone** smart shape.

13. On the **Drag and Drop** inspector, select the **Format** tab.

14. Click **Object Actions**.

15. On the **Accepted Drag Sources** dialog box, deselect everything except **Beer_Tee** and **Collared_Shirt**.

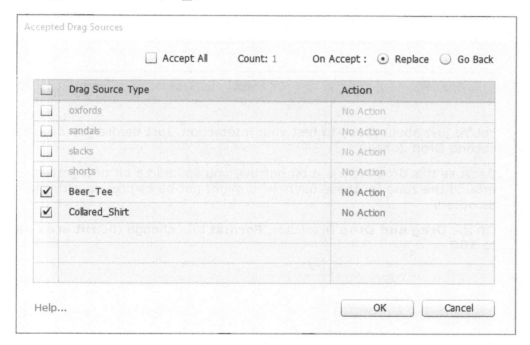

16. From the top of the dialog box, deselect **Accept All**.

17. Select **Replace**.

18. Click the **OK** button.

19. Repeat this process for the other two Drop Zones.

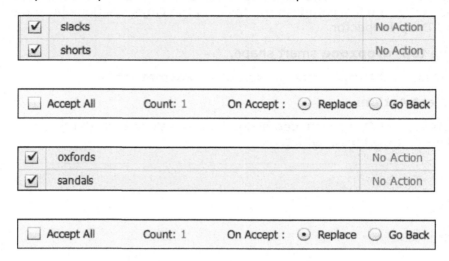

You're just about ready to test your interaction. Just before you do, select the second Drop Zone.

Because this drop zone is a bit narrow, you can add a bit of a grace area around the zone for those users who might not be as precise with the mouse as others.

20. On the **Drag and Drop** Inspector, **Format** tab, change the **Hit area padding** to **100**.

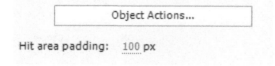

21. Preview the project.

22. Test the interaction.

23. Close the preview.

24. Save and Close project

Multi-State Objects

In the past, if you wanted to present multiple versions of an object to learners as they interacted with the lesson, you needed to add multiple objects to the slide, hide them, and then use advanced actions to make visible objects hide and hidden objects appear.

Adobe Captivate 9 supports multiple states, allowing you to develop interactive content without using multiple objects or the "hide and show" technique mentioned above. In addition, using states allows you to clean up what would otherwise be a cluttered, complicated project Timeline.

During the last activity and Confidence Check, you created a Drag and Drop Interaction. You'll enhance that interaction by changing the expression on James' face as you select his wardrobe.

Student Activity: Change Object States

1. Open **StateMe** from the Captivate9BeyondData folder.

2. Observe the Library.

   Notice that there are images in the Library representing James as sad, happy, and confused.

3. Create a New State.

   ☐ select slide **2** and, on the slide, select James' head

   ☐ on the **Properties Inspector**, click the **State View** button

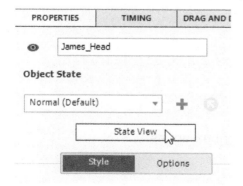

Adobe Captivate 9: Beyond The Essentials

The Object State view opens.

❑ at the left of the window, click **New State**

❑ change the name of the new state to **Happy**

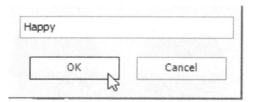

❑ click the **OK** button

4. Change the object used in a State.

❑ on the Properties Inspector, **Style** tab, click the button containing the words **James_RegularHead**

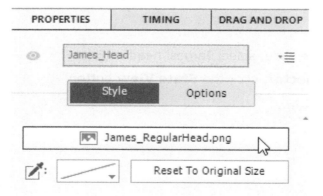

The **Select Image from Library** dialog box opens.

❑ from the list at the right, select **James_HappyHead**

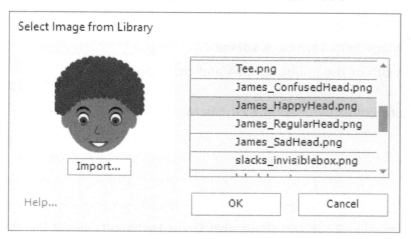

Select Image from Library

Tee.png
James_ConfusedHead.png
James_HappyHead.png
James_RegularHead.png
James_SadHead.png
slacks_invisiblebox.png

Import...

Help...   OK   Cancel

❑ click the **OK** button

Yikes! The new image is way too big!

5. Resize an image.

❑ with the image selected, click the **Options** tab on the **Properties Inspector**

❑ change W to **144** and the H to **148**

Transform

☐ Lock Size and Position

X: 202   Y: 39

W: 144   H: 148

☐ Constrain proportions

States Confidence Check

1. Create a New State named **Sad**.

2. Replace the image with **James_SadHead**.

3. Change the Width of the image to **144** and the Height to **148**.

4. Leave the State Editor by clicking **Exit State**.

Exit State

5. Still working on slide **2**, on the **Drag and Drop** Inspector, select the **Actions** tab.

6. From the first drop-down menu in the **On Success** area, choose **Change State of**.

7. Ensure the next drop-down menu has **James_Head** selected.

8. From the next drop-down menu, choose **Happy**.

9. Ensure **Continue Playing the project** is selected.

10. From the first drop-down menu in the **On Failure** area, choose **Change State of**.

11. Ensure the next drop-down menu has **James_Head** selected.

12. From the next drop-down menu, choose **Sad**.

13. Ensure **Continue Playing the project** is selected.

14. Preview the project.

15. If you drag the incorrect clothing to James and click the **How do I look** button, you should see James' expression change from **Happy** to **Sad**.

16. Close the preview.

17. Add another **New State** named **Confused**.

18. Replace the existing image with **James_ConfusedHead**.

19. Change the Width of the image to **144** and the Height to **148**.

20. Exit State View.

21. For the shirt Drop Zone, change the Action if the **collared shirt** is used to display James' happy face. (Hint: Format tab > Object Actions.)

22. Deselect **Continue Playing Project**.

Note: You deselected **Continue Playing Project** in the step above. During the past few activities, you've sometimes left this option on, and at other times you've deselected it. In the step above, deselecting the option allows James' expression to change and prevents the Drag and Drop interaction from telling the project to continue. If you had left **Continue Playing Project** on, the interaction completes and you won't be able to interact with the How Do I Look button as intended.

23. For the shirt Drop Zone, use the Object Actions button (Accepted Drag Sources dialog box) to change the Action if the **beer tee** is selected to display James' confused face.

| ✓ | Beer_Tee | Change State of | |
| ✓ | Collared_Shirt | Change State of | |

24. For the pants Drop Zone, use the Object Actions button to change the state of James' head for picking the shorts to **Confused**.

25. For the pants Drop Zone, use the Object Actions button to change the state of James' head for picking the pants to **Happy**.

26. For the shoes Drop Zone, use the Object Actions button to change the state of James' head for picking the sandals to **Confused**.

27. For the shoes Drop Zone, use the Object Actions button to change the state of James' head for picking the oxfords to **Happy**.

28. Preview the project, test the Interaction and the states.

29. Close the preview.

30. Save and close the project.

iCONLOGiC
"Skills and Drills" Learning

Module 8: Actions

In This Module You Will Learn About:

- Standard Actions, page 130
- Conditional Actions, page 146
- Multiple Decision Blocks, page 155

And You Will Learn To:

- Use a Completed Action, page 130
- Name Objects, page 133
- Create a Mask, page 135
- Control Object Visibility, page 136
- Create a Simple Advanced Action, page 137
- Attach an Action to a Button, page 140
- Group Timeline Objects, page 141
- Create a Variable, page 146
- Create a Conditional Action, page 150
- Create Decision Blocks, page 155

Standard Actions

If you want an interactive object (Button, Click Box, or Text Entry Box) to perform a single Action, it's a simple matter of selecting the object and visiting the Actions tab on the Properties Inspector. Common actions include jumping to a slide, playing a sound, or even opening a website or a file.

During the lessons that follow, you will create an interactive recipe that teaches a learner how to make Biff's famous caramel apples. Along the way you will use standard actions, conditional actions, and combo actions that provide the learner with an adjusted list of ingredients based on the number of caramel apples the learner wants to make. In addition, you'll set things up so that with a click of a button, learners are able to view images of the shopping list and the finished caramel apple.

Student Activity: Use a Completed Action

1. Open **ActionMe_Complete** from the Captivate9BeyondData folder.

   This project contains all of the actions that you will learn to create during this module.

2. Preview the project.

3. Click the **Shopping List** button at the bottom of the slide.

   A picture of each ingredient needed to create a caramel apple appears.

4. Click the **Caramel Apple** button.

The ingredients disappear and are replaced by the finished apple. Are you hungry yet?

5. Click the **Directions** button to move to the next slide.

6. Type a number between 1 and 7 into the desired servings text entry box and then click the **Update Recipe** button.

The amount of each ingredient changes to reflect the number of servings you requested.

Are you curious to learn what will happen if you enter **0** for the number of apples?

7. Type a **0** into the Desired Servings text entry box and click the **Update Recipe** button.

A caption appears indicating that using a value of 0 was not a good idea.

> Huh? Are you on a diet?
> Please enter a value greater than 0.

What if you need more than seven apples?

8. Enter a number larger than 7 for the desired servings and click the **Update Recipe** button.

A tip is displayed at the right (it's a Smart Shape) warning you about trying to melt too much caramel at a time.

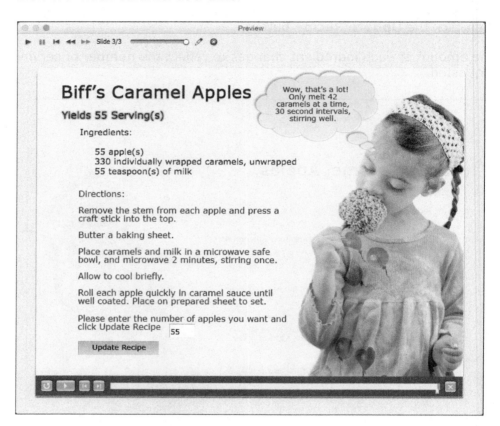

Did you notice that each time you clicked the Update Recipe button the Yield text below the title changed and glowed? If not, give it another try.

Now that you know what the recipe project looks like and how it should behave, you can get down to adding the actions required to make everything work. Because this project has the scenario fully implemented, you can return to this file at any time if you get stuck.

9. Close the preview.

10. Close the project without saving.

Student Activity: Name Objects

1. Open **SimpleActionMe** from the Captivate9BeyondData folder.

2. Name slide objects.

   ☐ go to slide **2**

   The slide is a mess. However, when the learner gets to this slide, the slide objects appear or disappear when the buttons are clicked.

   ☐ on the slide, double-click image of the **green apple**

   On the Properties Inspector, notice that the apple image has a nondescript name (Image_2). You will soon need to locate some of the images within a drop-down menu in the Advanced Actions dialog box. Naming an object makes that task easier.

   ☐ from the top of the Properties Inspector, change Name to **Apple** and press [**enter**]

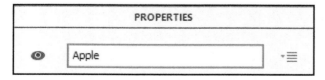

   At the far left of the Timeline, notice that the new name for the apple appears.

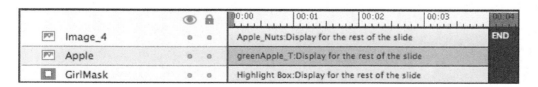

Naming Objects Confidence Check

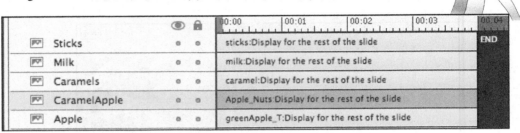

1. Give the remaining images names as follows:

   Image of popsicle sticks: **Sticks**

   Image of caramels: **Caramels**

   Image of quart of milk: **Milk**

   Image of finished caramel apple: **CaramelApple**

		👁	🔒	00:00	00:01	00:02	00:03	00:04
🖼	Sticks	⊙	⊙	sticks:Display for the rest of the slide				END
🖼	Milk	⊙	⊙	milk:Display for the rest of the slide				
🖼	Caramels	⊙	⊙	caramel:Display for the rest of the slide				
🖼	CaramelApple	⊙	⊙	Apple_Nuts:Display for the rest of the slide				
🖼	Apple	⊙	⊙	greenApple_T:Display for the rest of the slide				

2. Save your work.

   Note: You've spent a fair amount of time naming objects. I bet you're wondering if there's any real value to the endeavor. As you begin creating advanced actions and need to select objects from a drop-down menu containing dozens of objects, you will find that naming slides and slide objects pays huge dividends.

Student Activity: Create a Mask

1. Ensure that the **SimpleActionMe** project is still open.

2. Use a Highlight Box as a mask.

   ☐ ensure that you are still on slide **2**

   ☐ choose **View > Magnification > 50%**

   There is a large Highlight Box on the Pasteboard at the right.

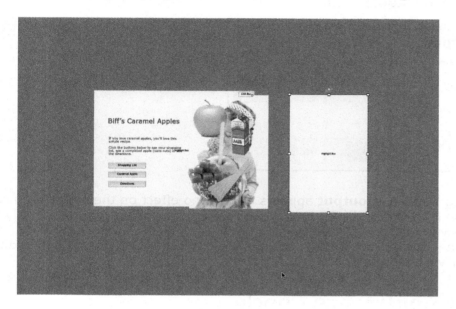

   Because Pasteboard objects neither Preview nor Publish, the Pasteboard is a great place to drop objects while you try to determine how or where you are going to use them.

   ☐ drag the Highlight Box onto the slide so that it covers the image of the little girl (you will use Actions in just a bit to make the Highlight Box hide the girl on the slide when the learner clicks a button)

   Notice that after you drag the Highlight Box (it has the name **GirlMask**) onto the picture of the girl, it automatically covers the girl but goes behind the other slide objects. This is caused by the vertical stacking order of the slide objects on the Timeline.

		👁	🔒	00:00	00:01	00:02	00:03	00:04
🖼	Sticks	●	●	sticks:Display for the rest of the slide				**END**
🖼	Milk	●	●	milk:Display for the rest of the slide				
🖼	Caramels	●	●	caramel:Display for the rest of the slide				
🖼	CaramelApple	●	●	Apple_Nuts:Display for the rest of the slide				
🖼	Apple	●	●	greenApple_T:Display for the rest of the slide				
⬜	GirlMask	●	●	Highlight Box:Display for the rest of the slide				

3. Save your work.

Student Activity: Control Object Visibility

1. Ensure that the **SimpleActionMe** project is still open.

    When you previewed the completed project (ActionMe_Complete), you might recall that the ingredients did not appear until after you clicked a button. The reason is simple enough: the **Visible in output** option.

2. Make the Apple image invisible in the output.

    ☐ select the **Apple** image

    ☐ on the Properties Inspector, to the left of the Name field, click **Visible in output**

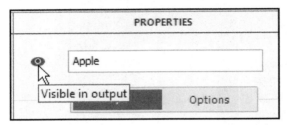

Clicking **Visible in output** appears to have no effect on the Apple—you can still see it on the slide. The visibility option controls if the object is visible to the learner in the *published* version of the lesson (the output). Although the Apple has been set to initially be invisible to the learner, it can be forced to appear via an Action.

Visibility Confidence Check

1. Select each of the remaining images (Sticks, Milk, Caramels, CaramelApple) and disable Visible in output.

    Note: You can control the visibility of multiple objects at one time. Select multiple objects by using [shift]-click and then click **Visible in output**.

2. Save your work.

Student Activity: Create a Simple Advanced Action

1. Ensure that the **SimpleActionMe** project is still open.

   If you want to make a single hidden image appear, that's easy. Select a button and, from the Actions tab of the Properties Inspector, choose **Show** from the **On Success** drop-down menu. Lastly, select an image from the **Show** drop-down menu.

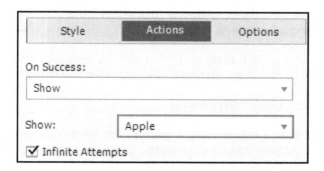

   But this is an advanced book, right? Your goal is to display *all* of the images that make up the ingredients at one time. To perform that bit of wizardry, you need to create an Advanced Action. It will be a simple Advanced Action, but an Advanced Action nevertheless.

2. Open the Advanced Actions dialog box.

   ❑ still working on slide **2**, choose **Project > Advanced Actions**

   The Advanced Actions dialog box opens.

3. Create an Action.

   ❑ from the **Action Type** drop-down menu, choose **Standard actions**

   ❑ in the **Action Name** field, type **displayShoppingList**

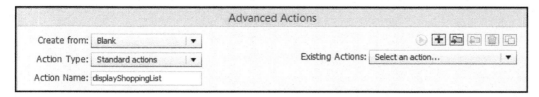

   ❑ in the **Actions** area, double-click the **first row**

   ❑ from the **Select Action** drop-down menu, choose **Show**

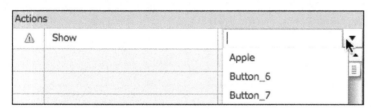

Notice that there is a yellow warning icon to the left of the Action. This is a visual indicator that the Action is not complete.

When you selected Show, a drop-down menu opened to the right. All of the objects in the project are represented in this list. Some of the objects have default item names assigned by Captivate (such as Text_Caption_11). It's a good bet that you don't know which caption is number 11. Thanks to the names you assigned the images a moment ago, you can see those objects by name in the menu. It is not necessary to name every object in a project. However, if you need to locate an object within a drop-down list (like now), giving it a unique and meaningful name is important.

You need to cover up the image of the little girl. You will do this by "showing" the Highlight Box (the Highlight Box has already been named **GirlMask**).

❑ from the drop-down menu, choose **GirlMask**

Notice that the warning sign at the left is now a green checkmark. The green checkmark indicates that the Action row is complete. Of course, the Action might be wrong, but at least the syntax is correct and complete.

❑ double-click in the **next row** in the **Actions** area

❑ from the **Select Action** drop-down menu, choose **Show**

Once again, notice the warning sign indicating that the Action is not yet complete.

❑ from the drop-down menu, choose **Apple**

The yellow warning sign turns into a green checkmark indicating that the Action is complete.

Simple Action Confidence Check

1. Add more rows to the Action that will show the Caramels, Milk, and Sticks.

   Ensure that all of the rows are green (indicating that each of the rows are complete).

Actions		
✔	Show	GirlMask
✔	Show	Apple
✔	Show	Caramels
✔	Show	Milk
✔	Show	Sticks

2. Click the **Save As Action** button and then click the **OK** button when notified of the successful save.

   One small piece of the action is missing. In the completed lesson, clicking the **Shopping List** button not only displayed all four ingredients but also hid the picture of the final product (the Caramel Apple). You need to insert one more line into the action for this to work.

3. Double-click the next available blank row and from the **Select Action** drop-down menu, choose **Hide**.

4. From the drop-down menu, choose **CaramelApple**.

5. Click the **Update Action** button and then click the **OK** button.

   Your Action should look like this:

Actions		
✔	Show	GirlMask
✔	Show	Apple
✔	Show	Caramels
✔	Show	Milk
✔	Show	Sticks
✔	Hide	CaramelApple

Note: Curious about what to do if you enter an erroneous Action line and need to remove it? Or perhaps you'd like to duplicate a line and save yourself some repetitive work? You'll find standard Cut, Copy, Paste, and Remove tools in the upper right of the Actions area in the dialog box. You will use some of these tools soon.

6. Click the **Close** button to close the Advanced Actions dialog box.

7. Save the project.

Student Activity: Attach an Action to a Button

1. Ensure that the **SimpleActionMe** project is still open.

   You have created an Action, but there is nothing in the project that is making the Action kick into, well, action. Next you will attach the Action to the **Shopping List** button on slide **2**.

   When a learner clicks the button, the Action "kicks in."

   ❑ on slide **2**, select the **Shopping List button**

   ❑ on the **Properties Inspector**, select the **Actions** tab

   ❑ from the **On Success** drop-down menu, choose **Execute Advanced Actions**

   ❑ from the **Script** drop-down menu, notice that **displayShoppingList** is selected (it's currently your only Advanced Action)

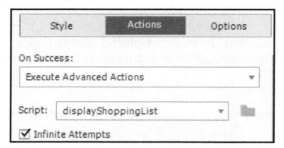

2. Preview the project and click the Shopping List button.

   The ingredients you need to purchase should appear, and the little girl should disappear.

   Note: If the Action does not work, first ensure you have attached the **displayShoppingList** Action to the **Shopping List** button as instructed in step 1 above. If that isn't the problem, choose **Project > Advanced Actions**. From the **Existing Actions** drop-down menu at the far right of the Advanced Actions dialog box, choose the **displayShoppingList** Action. The Action should look like the image below. If not, you can edit any value by double-clicking the value displayed and making a different choice from the drop-down menu.

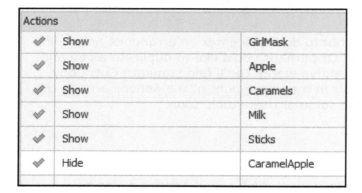

3. Close the preview, and then save and close the project.

Student Activity: Group Timeline Objects

1. Open the **SimpleActionMe_Step2** project from the Captivate9BeyondData folder.

   Did you find it tedious to have to Show each item in the shopping list one at a time as you built the Action? Wouldn't it be nice if you could Show all of the ingredients using just one command line in the Action? It's possible, assuming you have grouped the items in the shopping list together first.

   ☐ go to slide **2** and select all of the shopping list images (**Apple, Sticks, Milk, Caramels**)

   Note: You can select multiple objects by selecting one, pressing [**shift**] on your keyboard and then selecting the others.) Be careful not to select more of the slide objects than those mentioned above. Only four images should be selected.

   ☐ with the four images selected, choose **Edit > Group**

   The images are grouped not only on the slide but also on the Timeline. Because the **Visible in output** option was deselected for each of the selected items, the group is initially invisible to the learner.

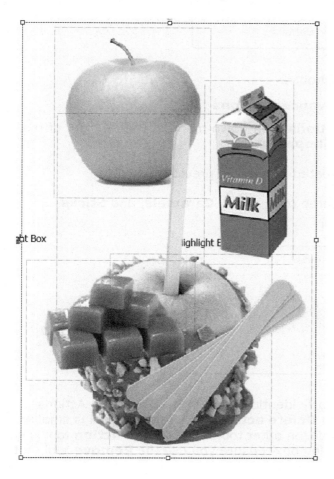

On the Timeline, the triangle to the left of the group name can be clicked to collapse or expand the group. The objects can still be manipulated individually, but also now work together as a group.

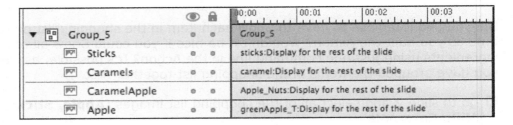

2. Name a group.

❏ on the Timeline, ensure that the group is selected

❏ on the Properties Inspector, change the group's Name to **ShoppingListGroup** and press [**enter**]

3. Remove lines from an Action.

❏ choose **Project > Advanced Actions**

❏ from the **Existing Actions** drop-down menu at the far right of the dialog box, choose **displayShoppingList**

This is the Action you created during the previous activity.

❏ select the following three rows: **Milk**, **Caramels**, and **Sticks**

❏ click the **Remove** tool

Note: There are two, nearly identical tools in the Advanced Actions dialog box: **Remove** and **Delete action**. The **Remove** tool is smaller and grouped with a half-dozen other tools. The **Delete action** tool is in the upper right of the dialog box. Ensure you use the **Remove** tool, not the **Delete action** tool.

4. Edit a line in the Action so that it uses the Group you created a moment ago.

   ❏ double-click the word **Apple**

   ❏ from the drop-down menu, choose **ShoppingListGroup**

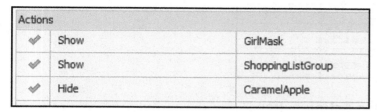

Actions		
✔	Show	GirlMask
✔	Show	ShoppingListGroup
✔	Hide	CaramelApple

   ❏ click the **Update Action** button (and click the **OK** button when prompted)

   ❏ click the **Close** button to close the Advanced Actions dialog box

   You need to create an Action for the **Caramel Apple** button. This Action is similar to the **Shopping List** button, but in reverse. Instead of showing all of the ingredients and then hiding the finished apple, you hide all of the ingredients and show the finished apple.

5. Duplicate an Action.

   ❏ on slide **2**, select the **Caramel Apple** button

   ❏ on the **Properties Inspector**, locate the **Actions tab**

   ❏ from the **On Success** drop-down menu, choose **Execute Advanced Actions**

   ❏ at the right of the Script drop-down menu click **Advanced Actions**

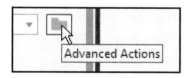

   Clicking Advanced Actions is an alternate method of getting to the Advanced Actions dialog box (**Project > Advanced Actions**).

   ❏ from the **Existing Actions** drop-down menu, choose **displayShoppingList**

   ❏ click the **Duplicate action** tool

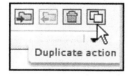

   The duplicate action is named **Duplicate_Of_displayShoppingList** by default.

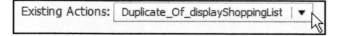

6. Rename an Action.

   ☐ in the **Action Name** field, change the name of the action to **displayCaramelApple**

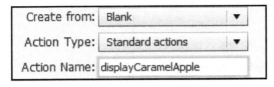

Create from:	Blank
Action Type:	Standard actions
Action Name:	displayCaramelApple

   ☐ click the **Update Action** button
   ☐ click the **OK** button

7. Edit the new Action.

   ☐ to the left of the **ShoppingListGroup** line, double-click the word **Show**

   The word changes to the Select Action drop-down menu.

   ☐ from the **Select Action** drop-down menu, choose **Hide**
   ☐ from the drop-down menu, choose **ShoppingListGroup**

| ✔ | Hide | ShoppingListGroup |

8. Update the Action.

   ☐ click the **Update Action** button
   ☐ click the **OK** button

Editing Actions Confidence Check

1. Edit the action to Show the **CaramelApple**.

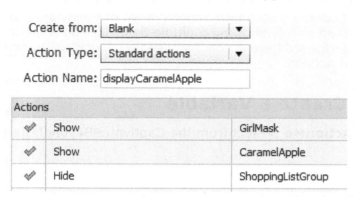

Create from:	Blank	▼
Action Type:	Standard actions	▼
Action Name:	displayCaramelApple	

Actions

✔	Show	GirlMask
✔	Show	CaramelApple
✔	Hide	ShoppingListGroup

2. Update the Action.

3. Close the Advanced Actions dialog box.

4. With the **Caramel Apple** button selected on the slide, select **displayCaramelApple** as the **Script** to Execute.

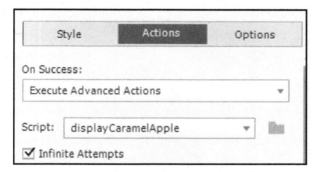

| Style | Actions | Options |

On Success:

Execute Advanced Actions   ▼

Script: displayCaramelApple   ▼

☑ Infinite Attempts

5. Save and preview the project.

6. During the preview, click back and forth between the **Shopping List** and **Caramel Apple** buttons.

    The images should switch back and forth on demand.

7. Close the preview.

8. Save and close the project.

Conditional Actions

I hope you agree that up to this point, Actions have been sweet... as sweet as a caramel apple. But let's crank things up a notch or two with a slightly more complex Action. The previous project contains Standard Actions, a list of behaviors. Advanced Actions are more powerful than simply allowing multiple behaviors on a single object interaction. They can also perform different actions based on specific situations. These are called Conditional Actions.

Student Activity: Create a Variable

1. Open the **ComplexActionMe** project from the Captivate9BeyondData folder.

2. Go to slide **3**.

   There is a **numberOfServings** variable just under the title, and there are other variables that display how much of each ingredient is needed.
   You calculate these values in a conditional action based on the number of servings the learner requests.

3. Drag the Text Caption and the Smart Shape from the Pasteboard to the slide and position the objects until your slide is similar to the picture below.

The Text Caption already has a name (**ZeroWarning**) and is not Visible in output. (You can confirm both by selecting the caption and observing the Properties Inspector.) Select the Smart Shape (the thought bubble) and notice that it is named **Tip** and is set to not be Visible in output. To manipulate the number of servings and the amount of each ingredient needed, you need to create a variable to store the learner input.

4. Create a Variable.

☐ choose **Project > Variables**

The Variables dialog box opens.

☐ from the **Type** drop-down menu, ensure **User** is selected

☐ click the **Add New** button and then type **servingsRequested** into the **Name** field

☐ in the **Value** field, type **1**

☐ in the **Description** field, type **The number of servings desired input by the learner. Should be greater than 0. Used in the advanced action updateRecipe.**

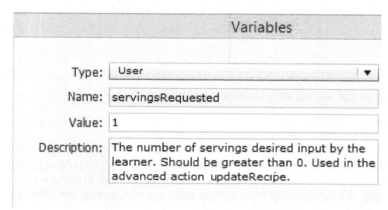

☐ click the **Save** button and then click the **Close** button

The new variable needs to be associated with the Text Entry Box so that when the learner types a number, the number is stored in the servingsRequested variable.

Once stored, the number can be displayed later in the lesson or used by an Advanced Action to perform calculations.

5. Associate the new variable with an object on the slide.

☐ still working on slide **3**, select the **Text Entry Box**

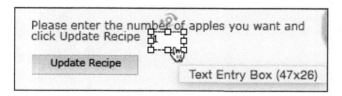

☐ on the **Properties Inspector**, select the **Style** tab

☐ from the **Variable** drop-down menu, select **servingsRequested**

6. Review the purpose for some of the other variables.

   ☐ choose **Project > Variables**

   You created one of the variables in the list (servingsRequested). Captivate comes with two user variables already created (cpQuizInfoStudentID and cpQuizInfoStudentName). Captivate automatically created another variable (**Text_Entry_Box_1**) when the Text Entry Box was inserted on the slide. I created the rest of the variables for you. Before proceeding, let's ensure that you understand the role of each of the variables in the Caramel Apple recipe.

   As I mentioned above, the first variable, **Text_Entry_Box_1**, was created by Captivate automatically when I inserted the Text Entry Box onto slide 3. The rest of the variables can be broken down into two categories: the number of items needed for a single caramel apple and the number of items necessary to meet the **servingsRequested** by the learner. To determine how much of an ingredient is necessary, Captivate needs both of these pieces of information.

   Text_Entry_Box_1
   appleUnit
   caramelUnit
   cpQuizInfoStudentID
   cpQuizInfoStudentName
   milkUnit
   numberOfApples
   numberOfCaramels
   numberOfServings
   numberOfSticks
   servingsRequested
   stickUnit
   teaspoonsOfMilk

Here is what the variables in the list do:

Single Serving Variables:

appleUnit: The number of apples for a single serving.

caramelUnit: The number of caramels for a single serving.

milkUnit: The number of teaspoons of milk for a single serving.

stickUnit: The number of sticks for a single serving.

Calculated Variables:

numberOfApples: The number of apples required for the desired servings of caramel apples.

numberOfCaramels: The number of caramels required for the desired servings of caramel apples.

teaspoonsOfMilk: The number of teaspoons of milk for the desired servings of caramel apples.

numberOfSticks: The number of sticks required for the desired servings of caramel apples.

numberOfServings: The number of servings of CaramelApples.

7. Close the Variables dialog box. Keep the project open.

Student Activity: Create a Conditional Action

1. Ensure that the **ComplexActionMe** project is still open.

   It is time to begin creating the Action that calculates the amount of each ingredient needed and that displays the proper messages for either zero servings or a large number of servings.

2. Create a Conditional Action.

   ❏ choose **Project > Advanced Actions**

   ❏ from the **Action Type** drop-down menu, choose **Conditional actions**

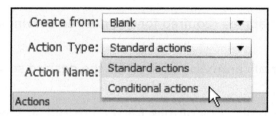

A conditional action contains three basic parts: a conditional check (IF area), a success case (Actions area within the IF area), and a failure case (Actions area within the ELSE area).

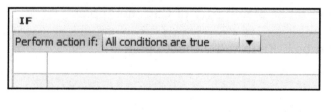

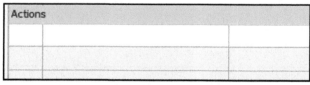

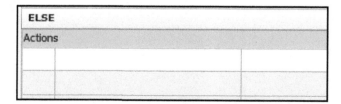

Here's how it works. If you were trying to decide what to do for lunch, you might go through a thought process like this:

```
IF

    is-it-lunchtime?(conditional check)

THEN

    drive to the nearest pizzeria(success case)
    order a giant pizza pie
    eat

ELSE

    keep working at my desk(failure case)

END
```

The condition is first evaluated. If the condition evaluates as TRUE, the behaviors in the success case are executed. Otherwise, the behaviors in the failure case are executed. The conditional check area may contain more than one item to check. For example, you may wish to check *is-it-lunchtime?* as well as *am-I-hungry?* You can evaluate both items and make a decision upon whatever combination of items you like. Perhaps you require that it be lunchtime AND that you are hungry to go out for pizza. Or maybe because you are hungry regardless of the time of day OR if it is lunchtime regardless if you are hungry, you should go out for pizza. To set this option within Captivate, you need to select the correct option from the **Perform action if** drop-down menu (just below the IF bar).

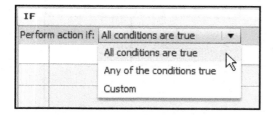

For this project, things are kept simple with just one condition to check.

3. Confirm the Perform action.

   ❑ from the **Perform action if** drop-down menu, verify that **All conditions are true** is selected.

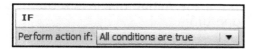

Before you start programming a conditional action, you should take a step back to analyze the goal of the action. The conditional action that you are about to create has three sections: (1) check if the servings requested is greater than 7, (2) check if the number of servings requested is a positive number and calculate ingredients and (3) show a glowing yield message. Often it is useful to sketch out a flowchart or jot down how you want the action to behave. A flowchart for this conditional action is shown below.

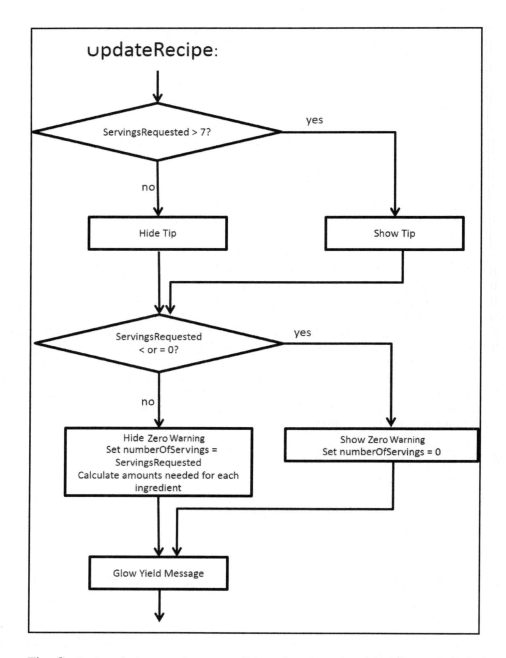

The first step is to create a conditional action that checks to see if the learner has input a serving size of at least 7. If so, the Action displays a tip message about how many caramels to melt at one time.

4. Create a conditional action.

   ❏ in the **Action Name** field, type **updateRecipe**

5. Create a conditional check.

   ❏ double-click in the first row of the **IF** area

   ❏ from the first drop-down menu, choose **variable** (the variable drop-down menu changes to a list of variables)

   ❏ select **servingsRequested** from the list of variables

❑ from the **Select comparison operator** drop-down menu, choose **is greater than**

❑ from the next drop-down, choose **literal**

❑ type **7** and then press [**enter**] on your keyboard

IF			
Perform action if:	All conditions are true	▼	
✔	servingsRequested	is greater than	7

A quick note on literals versus variables. A literal value is an exact value, such as the number **7**; an exact name, such as **Biff**; or even an exact phrase, such as "**Actions are fun!**" A variable is something that does not have a set value and can change, like the number of servings requested (making it variable).

6. Create a success case.

❑ double-click the first row in the **Actions** area

❑ from the **Select Action** drop-down menu, choose **Show**

❑ from the drop-down menu, choose **Tip**

Actions		
✔	Show	Tip

The update recipe button may be clicked many times. If the number of servings is not excessive, any tip remaining from the previous recipe update should be cleared (hidden). This is done in the ELSE area.

7. Create a failure case.

❑ click the word **ELSE** to expand the ELSE area

❑ double-click the first row in the **Actions** area

❑ from the **Select Action** drop-down menu, choose **Hide**

❑ from the drop-down menu, choose **Tip**

IF		
ELSE		
Actions		
✔	Hide	Tip

❑ click the **Save As Action** button

❑ click the **OK** button

❑ click the **Close** button

Conditional Actions Confidence Check

1. Still working in the **ComplexActionMe** project, slide **3**, attach the **updateRecipe** Action to the **Update Recipe** button.

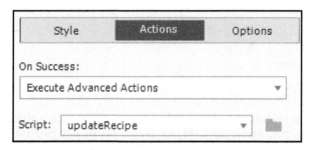

2. Preview the project.

3. Click the **Directions** button to move to slide **3**.

4. Type **22** into the Text Entry Box and then click the **Update Recipe** button.

   The **Tip** object should appear next to the little girl.

5. Type **3** into the Text Entry Box, and then click the **Update Recipe** button.

   The **Tip** object should disappear.

6. Close the preview.

7. Save your work.

Multiple Decision Blocks

A conditional action may contain numerous Decision Blocks. Each Decision Block contains a separate set of IF/ELSE areas. From a flow chart, decisions are represented by the diamond shape. For complicated Actions, the Decision Blocks can be named.

Student Activity: Create Decision Blocks

1. Ensure that the **ComplexActionMe** project is still open.

2. Name the Decision Blocks.

   ☐ choose **Project > Advanced Actions**

   ☐ from the **Existing Actions** drop-down menu, choose **updateRecipe**

   ☐ double-click the first word **Untitled** in the Decision Block area (it should be blue)

   ☐ change the name to **ExcessCheck** and then press [**enter**] on your keyboard

   ☐ double-click the word **Untitled** on the middle Decision Block

   ☐ change the name to **Calculate** and then press [**enter**] on your keyboard

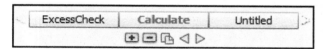

The word **Calculate** should still be blue indicating that you are editing that specific Decision Block.

3. Set up a Decision Block.

   ☐ double-click in the first row of the **IF** area

   ☐ choose **variable** from the first drop-down menu and then choose **servingsRequested**

   ☐ from the **Select comparison operator** drop-down menu, choose **lesser or equal to**

   ☐ from the **Variable** drop-down menu, choose **literal**

   ☐ type **0** and then press [**enter**]

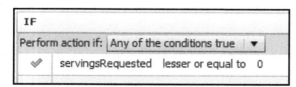

   ☐ in the **Actions** area, double-click in the first row

   ☐ from the **Select Action** drop-down menu, choose **Show**

   ☐ from the drop-down menu, choose **ZeroWarning**

Let's also set the numberOfServings variable now so that it displays correctly in the Yield Message.

❑ in the **Actions** area, double-click in the next blank row

❑ from the **Select Action** drop-down menu, choose **Assign**

❑ from the **Select Variable** drop-down menu, choose **numberOfServings**

❑ from the **Variable** drop-down menu, choose **literal**

❑ type a **0** and then press [**enter**]

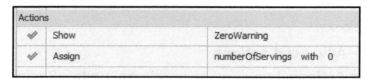

If the number of servings requested is more than 0, it is time to create all of the calculations that are displayed in the recipe text caption. For each ingredient, you will multiply the number of that ingredient necessary for a single serving (*ingredient*Unit) by the number of servings desired (servingsRequested) and save that into the total amount for that ingredient (numberOf*Ingredient*).

4. Create a failure case.

☐ click the word **ELSE** to expand the ELSE section

☐ double-click in the **Actions** area

☐ from the **Select Action** drop-down menu, choose **Hide**

☐ from the drop-down menu, choose **ZeroWarning**

☐ double-click in the next row and, from the **Select Action** drop-down menu choose **Assign**

☐ from the **Select Variable** drop-down menu, choose **numberOfServings**

☐ from the **Variable** drop-down menu, choose **variable**

☐ from the drop-down menu, choose **servingsRequested**

☐ double-click in the next row and, from the **Select Action** drop-down menu, choose **Expression**

☐ from the drop-down menu, choose **numberOfApples**

☐ from the **Variable** drop-down menu, choose **variable**

☐ from the drop-down menu, choose **appleUnit**

☐ from the **+** drop-down menu, choose *****

☐ from the **Variable** drop-down menu, choose **variable**

☐ from the drop-down menu, choose **servingsRequested**

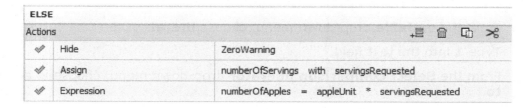

	ELSE	
	Actions	
✔	Hide	ZeroWarning
✔	Assign	numberOfServings with servingsRequested
✔	Expression	numberOfApples = appleUnit * servingsRequested

5. Click the **Update Action** button.

6. Click the **OK** button.

7. Click the **Close** button to close the Action.

8. Save and close the project.

Decision Blocks Confidence Check

1. Open the **ComplexActionMe_Part2** project from the Captivate9BeyondData folder.

   You are just about done. The last thing left to do is add the little glow effect to the Yield text. There are two choices here. The effect could be added to both the IF and the ELSE clauses of the Calculate decision block, but that seems inefficient because that would require you to add the same action in two places. It makes more sense to do it just once in its own decision block, one that is executed after the Calculate decision block.

2. Open the Advanced Actions dialog box.

3. Display the **UpdateRecipe** action.

4. On the Decision block list, **double-click** the third block and change the name to **Glow**.

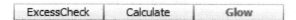

| ExcessCheck | Calculate | Glow |

   Adding this line is just a standard Action. The only way to incorporate a standard action into a conditional action is to create a condition that is always true. Any statement that can never fail is acceptable to use here.

5. Within the **IF** block, double-click the first blank line to select it.

6. From the **variable** drop-down menu, choose **literal**.

7. Type **1** into the text field.

8. From the **Select comparison operator** drop-down menu, choose **is equal to**.

9. Select **literal** from the **variable** drop-down menu.

10. Type **1** in the text field.

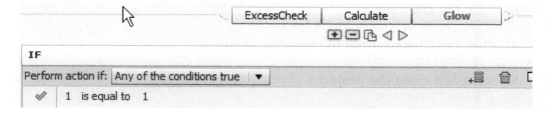

11. Select the **Glow** block.

    The action looks a little silly, but this is how you can get Captivate to execute a set of standard actions from within the conditional action type of advanced action. As many standard statements as needed can be inserted into the success case, and they will always be executed because 1 is *always* equal to 1.

12. Double-click in the first row of the actions area.

13. From the **Select Action** drop-down menu, choose **Apply Effect**.

14. From the drop-down menu, choose **YieldMessage**.

15. From the **Select Effect** drop-down menu, choose **Custom > GlowTwice**.

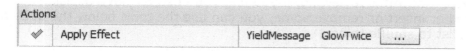

Note: The project you are working in is a legacy project created in an older version of Captivate. In Captivate 9, GlowTwice is not an available effect. When this project was upgraded to Captivate 9, the GlowTwice effect was retained but moved to the Custom list. If you start a Captivate 9 project from scratch, the GlowTwice effect will not be available for you to use unless you export it from this project and then import it.

16. Click **Update Action** to save the action.

Before you leave the Advance Action, look at the preview of your script by clicking the **Preview Action** button in the upper right of the dialog box.

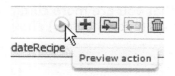

This option is available only for conditional actions. It doesn't make any sense for standard actions because you can see an entire standard action on one screen and use your scroll bar if you have a large number of action statements. However, for a conditional action, which may contain numerous decision blocks, this feature is pretty cool (at least to the geek in all of us).

It is a good idea at this point to compare this code structure to the flow chart on page 152. After reviewing, if you find you need to move decision blocks around or insert or remove some, you can use the tools below the decision block list to shuffle things.

17. Close the Preview Actions dialog box.

18. Close the Advanced Actions dialog box.

19. Save your work and preview the project.

20. When finished previewing the project, close the preview.

Are you wondering why there is a slide **1** in the project that seems to have little value? And are you wondering how the images were hidden when the rewind button on the playbar was clicked? These two items go hand in hand. I created an Advanced Action called **reset**. Now that you are more comfortable with Advanced Actions, the role of the reset action (shown below) should make sense.

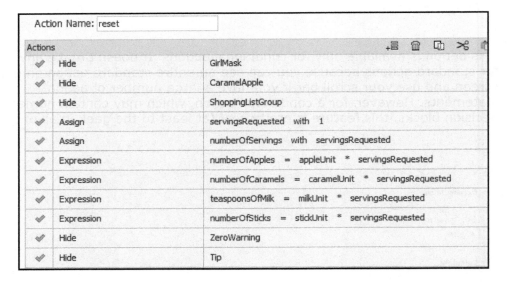

The **reset** action is executed upon entry to slide **2**. This is done on the Properties Inspector using the On Enter behavior in the Actions tab.

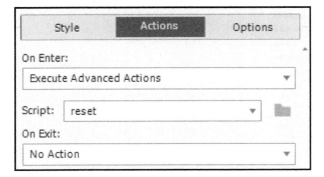

Now, about that first slide....

21. On the Timeline for slide **1**, notice that the slide is set to play for only a fraction of a second.

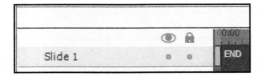

When you try to use an On Enter behavior on the first slide of a project, you don't always get the desired behavior. Creating a placeholder slide is a simple workaround. Making the second slide in a project behave as if it were the first slide ensures that the On Enter behavior is executed properly. Slide 1 in this case is simply a placeholder slide that has the same background as the second slide. The first slide plays for just a split second, which is not noticeable to the learner.

Note: When using this technique, be sure to remove any slide transitions so it appears as if two slides are just a single slide.

22. When you are done exploring your final project, save and close it.

Notes

_____

_____

_____

_____

_____

_____

_____

_____

_____

_____

_____

_____

_____

_____

_____

_____

_____

_____

_____

_____

_____

_____

_____

_____

_____

_____

_____

_____

_____

_____

_____

_____

_____

iCONLOGiC
"Skills and Drills" Learning

Module 9: Masters, Themes, and Templates

In This Module You Will Learn About:

And You Will Learn To:

Master Slides

If you need to add common objects to your slides (such as images or background colors), master slides are just the ticket. Instead of manually copying and pasting common objects onto slides, you can add them to a master slide. After that, it's a simple matter of applying the master slide to selected Filmstrip slides. Each new Adobe Captivate project contains one Main Master Slide and multiple Content Master Slides. You can format the Main Master Slide, format the existing Content Master Slides, or create your own Content Master Slides.

Student Activity: Work With the Main Master Slide

1. Open **MasterMe** from the Captivate9BeyondData folder.

2. Copy an image from slide 1 for use on a Master Slide.

   ☐ on the Filmstrip, select slide **1**

   ☐ right-click the "S" logo on the slide and choose **Copy**

3. Open the Master Slide Panel.

   ☐ choose **Window > Master Slide**

   The Filmstrip is replaced with the Master Slide panel. The first slide, and the largest, is the Main Master Slide. The remaining slides are the Content Master Slides.

   ☐ on the Master Slide panel, select the **Main Master Slide**

   ☐ choose **Edit > Paste**

   The logo shows up on the Main Master Slide and on *every* Content Master Slide.

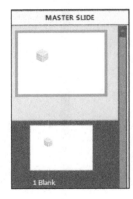

4. Exit the Master.

   ☐ on the toolbar at the top of the Captivate window, click **Exit Master**

   The logo appears on *every* Filmstrip slide. If you want an object to appear in the same location on every slide throughout the project, adding it to the Main Master Slide works great. Because the Main Master Slide affects every slide in the project, its most common use is for background colors and/or images. Pasting the logo on the Main Master Slide is overkill. Next you'll learn how to work with the Content Masters, which can be applied to individual or multiple Filmstrip slides.

5. Return to the Master Slide panel (**Window > Master Slide** or, on the Properties Inspector, click the **Master slide view** button).

6. Delete the logo from the Main Master Slide and then exit the Master.

Student Activity: Work With Content Masters

1. Ensure that the **MasterMe** project is still open.

2. Return to the Master Slide panel (**Window > Master Slide**).

3. Insert a Content Master Slide.

   ❏ choose **Insert > Content Master Slide**

   A new Content Master Slide is added after the existing Content Master named Blank.

4. Name the new Content Master Slide.

   ❏ with the new Content Master Slide selected, use the Properties Inspector to name the Content Master Slide **LogoLowerRight**

   On the Master Slide panel, the new Content Master Slide should now display the LogoLowerRight name.

5. Add the logo to the new Content Master Slide.

    ☐ right-click the **LogoLowerRight** Content Master Slide and choose **Edit > Paste**

    The logo that you copied earlier should appear on the LogoLowerRight Content Master. If not, Exit the Master, copy the logo on Filmstrip slide 1, return to the LogoLowerRight Content Master, and paste again.

6. Drag the logo to the lower right of the LogoLowerRight Content Master Slide.

7. Exit the Master.

    Because you have not yet applied the LogoLowerRight master to any of the Filmstrip slides, none of the Filmstrip slides are displaying the logo in the lower right.

8. Save your work.

Student Activity: Apply a Master to Filmstrip Slides

1. Ensure that the **MasterMe** project is still open.

2. Apply a Content Master Slide to Filmstrip slides.

    ❑ on the Filmstrip, select slide **2**

    Notice that slide **2** does not yet have the logo you added to the LogoLowerRight Content Master Slide. That will change the instant you apply the LogoLowerRight Content Master Slide to this (or any) Filmstrip slide.

    ❑ ensure that slide 2 is still selected
    ❑ press the [**shift**] key on your keyboard
    ❑ select slide **9**
    ❑ release the [**shift**] key

    Slides **2** through **9** should now be selected.

    ❑ on the Properties Inspector, select **LogoLowerRight** from the Master Slide drop-down menu

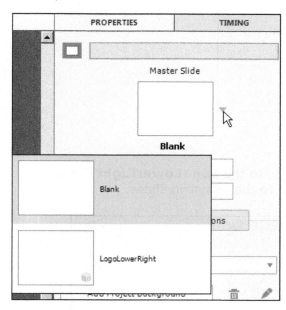

    The **LogoLowerRight** Content Master Slide is applied to the selected Filmstrip slides. When you go from slide to slide, you'll see the logo in the lower right corner of every slide (except the first and last slide).

3. Save your work.

Student Activity: Edit a Master

1. Ensure that the **MasterMe** project is still open.

2. Return to the Master Slide panel.

3. Reposition the logo on the **LogoLowerRight** Master Slide.

   ☐ on the Master Slide panel, select the **LogoLowerRight** Content Master
   ☐ select the **logo**
   ☐ on the **Properties Inspector**, select the Options tab
   ☐ from the **Transform** area, change the **X** value to **523**
   ☐ change the **Y** value to **366**

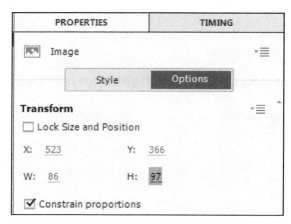

4. Exit the Master.

   Notice that the change you made to the **LogoLowerRight** Content Master Slide has instantly been applied to the Filmstrip slides.

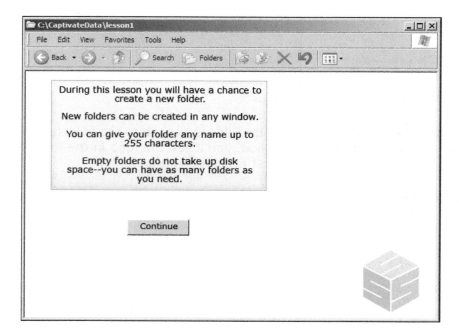

Masters Confidence Check

1. Return to the Master Slide panel.

2. Select the LogoLowerRight Content Master Slide and choose **Edit > Duplicate**.

   There should be two Content Master Slides named LogoLowerRight.

3. Rename the newest LogoLowerRight Content Master Slide as **Logo and Copyright**.

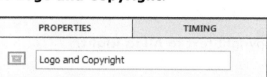

4. With the **Logo and Copyright** Content Master Slide selected, insert a text caption.

5. Delete the placeholder text from the new caption.

6. On the Properties Inspector, click the **Insert Symbol** tool.

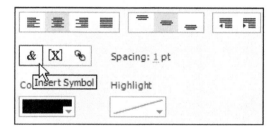

7. Select **Copyright** from the list of symbols.

8. Type **2016, All Rights Reserved** after the copyright symbol.

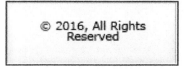

9. Using the Properties Inspector, change the Caption Type to **transparent** and change the Font to **Verdana**, **10 pt**.

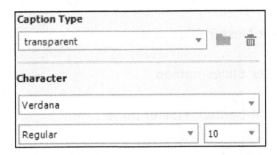

10. Change the alignment of the copyright text to **Align Right**.

11. Position the logo and the copyright notice in the lower right of the master slide (similar to the image below).

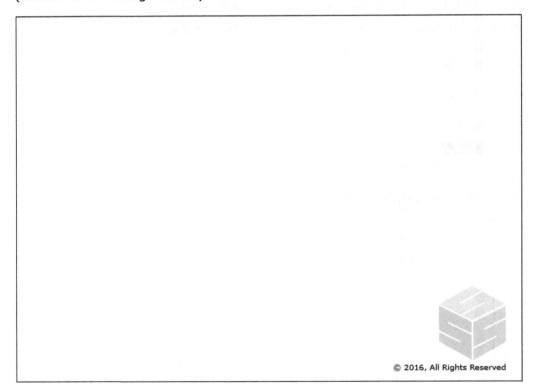

© 2016, All Rights Reserved

12. Exit the Master.

13. Apply the **Logo and Copyright** Master Slide to project Slides 2 through 9. (You learned how to do this on page 165.)

14. Save your work and close the project.

Themes

You've learned how masters can help ensure consistent placement of repetitive slide objects earlier in this module. Because masters can neither create nor design themselves, you'll appreciate the power of Themes. A Theme is a collection of pre-designed and positioned slide elements, master slides, object styles, and skins designed to give your project a consistent look and feel. Captivate ships with several Themes. You can edit and save the provided Themes, or you can create your own. You can choose to apply a theme to a new project or apply a Theme to any existing project at any time.

Student Activity: Apply a Theme

1. Open **ThemeMe** from the Captivate9BeyondData folder.

2. Go from slide to slide and notice that this project has ample content, but the overall look and feel of the project leaves plenty to be desired.

3. Apply a Theme to the project.

   ❑ click the **Themes** tool on the toolbar (not the Themes menu) and choose the **Clear** theme

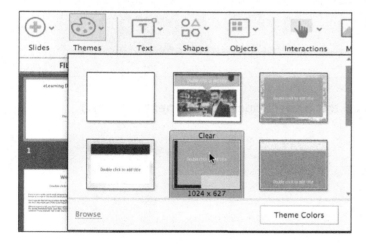

   Because the Object Styles used in each Theme look different, you are asked to confirm the action.

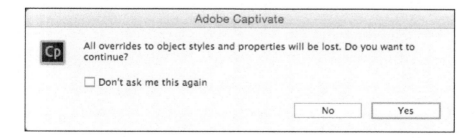

   ❑ click the **Yes** button

   After a few seconds, a bit of magic takes place and every slide in the project is formatted to match the Theme.

Themes Confidence Check

1. Spend a few moments applying some of the other available Themes to the project.

2. Apply the **Chic** theme to the project.

3. Save your work. (Keep the project open for the next activity.)

Student Activity: Create a Custom Theme

1. Ensure that the **ThemeMe** project is open and that you're using the **Chic** theme.

2. Go to slide **2**.

   Notice that there is a subtitle placeholder on the slide that is not being used by any of the slides in the project. Because it's not needed, you'll get rid of it next.

3. Open the Master Slide panel.

4. Edit a Content Master Slide.

   ❑ select the **Content 07** Content Master

   There are three placeholders on the master: one for the title, one for the subtitle, and one for the placeholder for the caption text. (You can insert placeholders via Insert > Placeholder Objects.)

   ❑ right-click the subtitle placeholder and choose **Delete**

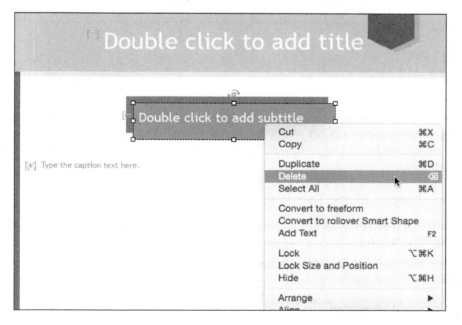

   ❑ click **OK** when prompted to confirm the deletion

5. If necessary, also delete the green smart shape from the slide.

6. Resize and reposition the caption placeholder on the master slide similar to the image below.

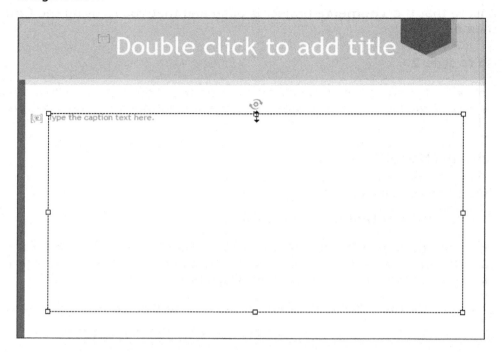

7. Exit the Master.

8. On the Filmstrip, select slide **2**.

   With just a few changes to a single master slide used by the Chic Theme, the text has been moved up on every slide. Although the current Theme is only slightly different from the original, it's still worth saving the updated theme as a new theme.

9. Save the changes to the Theme as a new Theme.

   ❑ from the **Themes** menu (not the Themes tool on the toolbar), choose **Save Theme As**

   ❑ name the theme **YourFirstNameTheme** and save it to the Captivate9BeyondData folder

   ❑ click the **OK** button to acknowledge the successfully saved Theme

10. Observe your Theme in the Themes panel.

☐ choose **Themes**

Your Theme appears on the Themes panel along with the original Themes. It can now be used by any new project or any existing project.

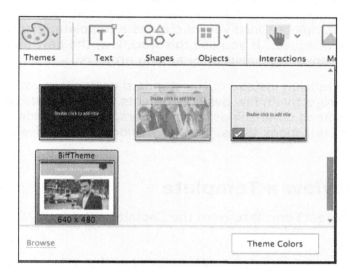

11. Apply a different theme to the ThemeMe project.

12. Apply your custom theme to the ThemeMe project.

13. Save and close the project.

Templates

To ensure that your projects are consistent from developer to developer, it's a good idea to use Themes (see page 171). As you have already seen earlier in this module, themes include professionally designed master slides, object styles, and placeholders that you can quickly apply to an entire project. But to ensure that each new project that you create is set to a specific size and contains specific objects in specific locations, you should create a template. Once you've created a template, you can use it when you create each new project. If you use this workflow, the new project looks exactly like the template, ensuring consistency among projects.

Templates, which use a **cptl** extension instead of the standard **cptx** extension, can be as simple as a single-slide project with few design elements. Or templates can be complex projects containing, among other things, placeholders, Filmstrip slides, heavily designed master slides, questions slides, variables, widgets, and advanced actions.

Student Activity: Review a Template

1. Open **Finished_S3_ProjectTemplate** from the Captivate9BeyondData folder.

   Notice that the project's name includes a **cptl** extension (this extension is used only by Captivate templates).

2. Ensure you are on slide **1**.

   There is a strange object on slide 1... a gray box containing the words "Text Animation." This is a Placeholder. When this template is used as the basis of a new project, you are able to replace the placeholder with the text for the Text Animation. The slide position, animation, font, and font size have already been determined by the person who created the template.

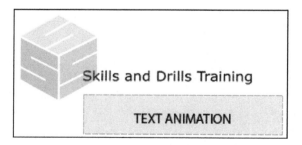

3. Go to slide **2**.

   Slide 2 is a Recording Slide Placeholder. When the template is used by a Captivate developer to create a new project, the developer is able to double-click the placeholder and immediately begin recording screen actions.

4. Review some of the Object Styles used in the template.

   ☐ choose **Edit > Object Style Manager**

   The template includes several custom Object Styles. SSS Default Text Caption is also set to be the default caption used whenever a caption is inserted onto a slide.

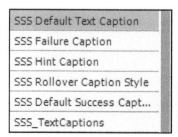
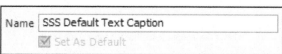

   ☐ click the **Cancel** button

5. Open the Master Slide panel.

   The template includes two custom Content Master Slides: **LogoLowerRight** and **Logo and Copyright**. You learned how to create these kinds of master slides on page 165.

6. Exit the Master.

7. Review the Skin.

   ☐ choose **Project > Skin Editor**

   The template is using a custom skin complete with a playbar with colors edited to match the colors on the clock background.

8. Close the Skin Editor.

9.   Review the Project Information.

❏ choose **File > Project Info**

The information about Super Simplistic Solutions has already been filled in. When the template is used as a project, all that the developer needs to do is update the fields.

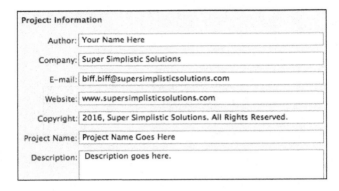

Project: Information	
Author:	Your Name Here
Company:	Super Simplistic Solutions
E-mail:	biff.biff@supersimplisticsolutions.com
Website:	www.supersimplisticsolutions.com
Copyright:	2016, Super Simplistic Solutions. All Rights Reserved.
Project Name:	Project Name Goes Here
Description:	Description goes here.

10.   Review the Start and End properties.

❏ from the left of the Preferences dialog box, select **Start and End**

Notice that a Preloader has already been specified. In addition, the Preloader % is already set to 50%. At the bottom of the dialog box, notice the **Fade** and **Project End options** have also been set.

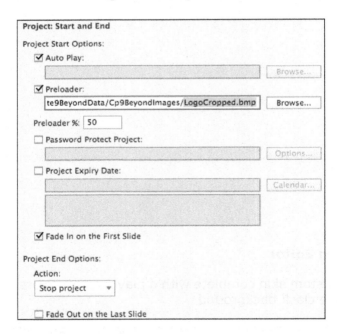

❏ click the **Cancel** button

This template looks pretty much ready to go. All you need to do is create a new project that uses the template, and you'll be off to the races.

11.   Close the template (do not save any changes if prompted).

Student Activity: Base a Project on a Template

1. Create a new project based on an existing template.

   ☐ choose **File > New Project > Project From Template**

   The Open dialog appears. You'll need to help Captivate find a Captivate template.

   ☐ navigate to the **Captivate9BeyondData** folder and open the **Finished_S3_ProjectTemplate**

   A moment ago you spent some time looking at different aspects of the template. The extension used by the template is **cptl**. Check out the name of this project: it's an untitled project with a **cptx** extension. When you open the template via Project From Template, the resulting file is a standard Captivate project that is an identical copy of the template. Unlike some programs that use templates, there is not a link (or relationship) between the template and the project. If you were to reopen the template, the change made to the template would not be reflected in any project(s) based on the template. Conversely, any changes made to a project have no effect on the template used to create it.

2. Replace a Text Animation Placeholder with text.

   ☐ on slide 1, double-click the TEXT ANIMATION placeholder

   The words "Replace Me" appear.

   ☐ double-click the words **Replace Me**

   The Text Animation Properties dialog box opens. Notice that the Font has already been set to Verdana and that the Size is 36. All you need to do is replace the content and not worry about how to insert a Text Animation, how to format it, or how to set its Properties.

   ☐ replace the words "Replace Me" with **Templates=Awesome**

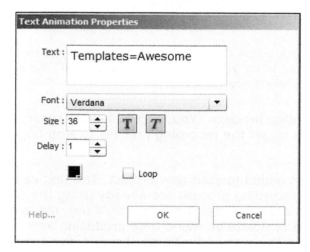

   ☐ click the **OK** button

3. Record a series of screen actions using the Recording Slide Placeholder.

   ☐ go to slide **2**

   ☐ double-click the words **Double-click to start recording**

   The untitled project disappears, and you are taken into Captivate's recording mode.

   ☐ select any program you like from the drop-down menu (I'm using Notepad in the image below... if nothing is available, create a recording of your desktop or start an application to capture)

   ☐ ensure that **Snap to Window** is selected

   ☐ from the **Recording Type** area, ensure **Automatic** is selected

   ☐ from the **Mode** drop-down menu, ensure **Demo** is selected

   ☐ **Panning** should be set to **No Panning** and **Audio** set to **No Narration**

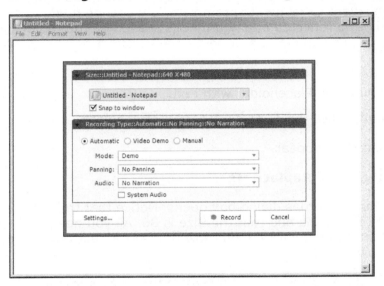

   ☐ click the **Record** button

4. After the 3-2-1 countdown, click a few things in the application you elected to record. (It really doesn't matter what you click because you won't be keeping the recording for more than a few more minutes.)

5. When finished, stop the recording process. (You learned how to record a software simulation—and how to get the recording process to stop beginning on page 7.)

   The recorded slides have been added to your new project. The text captions that were created during the recording process are already using the SSS Default Text Caption set up in the template. Nice! You could now move on and record more lessons using the template or spend time producing and publishing this lesson. Because this was just a demo showing how to use a Captivate template, you won't be saving this project.

6. Close the project without saving.

Student Activity: Create a Project Template

1. Create a new project template.

   ☐ **File > New Project > Project Template**

   The New Project Template dialog box opens. This is where you set up the width and height of the template. Once you select a width and height, all of the projects and screen recordings you create with the template will use this size.

   ☐ from the **Select** drop-down menu, choose **640 x 480**

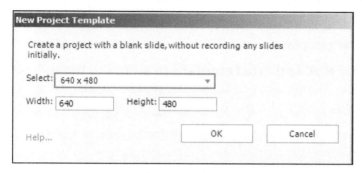

   ☐ click the **OK** button

   An untitled template opens. Notice that the file contains a **cptl** extension just like the template you opened and used earlier.

2. Save the project template to the Captivate9BeyondData folder as **MyCaptivateTemplate**.

3. Apply the Blank Theme to the template.

   ☐ choose **Themes > Blank**

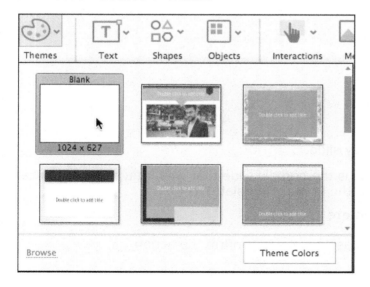

   ☐ click the **Yes** button on the alert dialog box

4. Copy a slide from a Captivate project into a Captivate Template.

   ❏ open **TemplateMe** from the Captivate9BeyondData folder.

   This is a 10-slide project that has been approved by SSS management. You'll be copying some of the assets in this approved project and pasting them into the new Project Template.

   ❏ select slide **1** on the Filmstrip

   ❏ choose **Edit > Copy**

   The slide has been copied to your computer's clipboard. It can now be pasted into the template.

5. Paste the slide into the template.

   ❏ click the tab for the **MyCaptivateTemplate** to switch to the template

   ❏ choose **Edit > Paste**

   The slide has been added to MyCaptivateTemplate.

6. Delete an unnecessary slide.

   ❏ select slide **1** (this is the original slide that was included automatically when you created the Project Template)

   ❏ choose **Edit > Delete**

   A dialog box appears asking you to confirm the action.

   ❏ click the **OK** button

   The **MyCaptivateTemplate** should now contain just the TOC slide you copied from the TemplateMe project.

Template Confidence Check

1. Ensure that the **MyCaptivateTemplate** and **TemplateMe** projects are still open.

2. Switch back to the **TemplateMe** project.

3. Copy and paste the last slide (Congrats) from the **TemplateMe** project to the **MyCaptivateTemplate**.

4. Switch to the **TemplateMe** project and display the Master Slide panel.

5. Select and **copy** both the **LogoLowerRight** and **Logo and Copyright** Content Master Slides to the clipboard.

6. Switch to the **MyCaptivateTemplate** and display the Master Slide panel.

7. Paste both master slides onto the Master Slides panel.

8. Close the TemplateMe project. (Leave MyCaptivateTemplate open.)

Template Placeholders

You can add any object to a template's slide including text captions, buttons, click boxes, and highlight boxes. When you add a text caption to a template, a typical process would be to insert some default text into the caption, such as "Title-Replace with your own text" or "Subhead-Replace with your own text." Developers who create projects using the template would be expected to replace the default text with actual text. However, if the developer neglects to replace the default text, the project will publish with any default text that is not actually replaced.

You can also add template placeholders for images, Text Captions, Rollover Images, and/or Rollover Captions, Text Animations and Animations, Recording Slides and Question Slides, Slide Videos, Smart Shapes, and Content Placeholders.

Student Activity: Insert a Placeholder

1. Ensure that **MyCaptivateTemplate** is still open.

2. Insert a Recording Slide Placeholder.

   ☐ on the Filmstrip, select slide **1**

   ☐ choose **Insert > Placeholder Slides > Recording Slide Placeholder**

Your new template is well on its way. What's left to do? You still need to create your object styles, set up the Project Info, set the Start and End preferences, and work on your Skin. And if you're planning to use Advanced Actions and Variables, it would be ideal to include them in the template. One final note about templates: if you've already created a project that contains all of these components, you can shortcut the whole template development phase by choosing **File > Save as** and choosing **Captivate Template Files** from the Save as type drop-down menu.

3. Save and close the template.

Module 10: Responsive Projects

In This Module You Will Learn About:

- Being Responsive, page 186
- Creating Responsive Projects, page 191
- Editing a Responsive Project, page 194
- Positioning Objects, page 201
- Responsive Styles, page 204

And You Will Learn To:

- Review a Responsive Project, page 186
- Customize Breakpoints, page 188
- Customize Theme Colors, page 191
- Use the Position Inspector, page 194
- Modify a Single Breakpoint, page 197
- Exclude from View, page 198
- Add a New Breakpoint, page 200
- Position and Link Objects, page 201
- Edit Breakpoint Object Styles, page 204

Being Responsive

The sale of smartphones is exceeding the sale of traditional phones; the sale of Tablet Portraits exceeds those of desktop computers. This trend has led to a need for eLearning developers to create courses that can be accessed from both Mobile Portrait and desktop devices.

The size of the screen that learners use to access eLearning lessons can vary widely. Consider the size of a typical smart phone compared to the various shapes and sizes of tablets, such as the Apple iPad, Microsoft Surface, and Amazon Kindle Fire. You could develop several Captivate projects that contain the same content but are sized to work on specific devices; however, you'd have to edit and update several projects! Who wants to do that? Additionally, who could possibly consider every screen size for every device? Even if you could build lessons for every screen size known today... what about the screen sizes for devices that have yet to be invented?

As an alternative to managing multiple Captivate projects, you can create a single, responsive project that provides optimal viewing, and an effective learning experience, across a wide range of devices and screen sizes.

Responsive design is an approach to development that allows for flexible layouts and flexible images and assets. Although the word **responsive** was traditionally used for building web pages, with Captivate, responsive design can be used to develop eLearning courses that detect the learner's screen size and orientation, and automatically change what the learner sees.

During this module, you'll learn how to navigate Captivate's responsive interface (which is very different than working in a standard project) and how to create responsive projects from scratch.

Student Activity: Review a Responsive Project

1. Open **ResponsiveScenarioMe** from the Captivate9BeyondData folder.

2. Preview the project.

   When you preview a responsive project, you are taken into an HTLM5 browser window. There are three buttons (**Breakpoints**) at the top of the preview window. (A Breakpoint is the point at which the layout changes size to accommodate a different screen size.)

   When clicked, the buttons display the eLearning lesson at different screen sizes. The three Breakpoints in this project are 1024, 768, and 360. The person who developed this project set these Breakpoints based on the devices their learners were anticipated to use. The Breakpoints represent a desktop or laptop user (1024), a Tablet Portrait user (768), and a Mobile Portrait user (360). When developing responsive projects, it is up to you to set the most common Breakpoints for your learners.

   Note: Responsive layouts are a new technology, and screen objects can display differently from browser to browser (or not at all). You should preview your courses in multiple browsers.

3. View the lesson at different screen sizes using the Breakpoints.

   ☐ with the preview window still open, click the **768** Breakpoint

   Rather than simply resizing the screen objects so they fit on the smaller screen, the layout automatically responds to accommodate the available real estate.

   ☐ click the **360** Breakpoint

   The preview at this Breakpoint is even more dramatic. A learner using a device this small would see something different than someone using a 1024 or 768 screen size, even though the content is the same.

4. Preview additional screen sizes.

   ☐ at the top of the preview window, below the Breakpoints, drag the slider left or right

   As you drag the slider, the preview changes to show how the lesson will look on just about any screen size available today. In addition, the screen size is displayed in the middle of your canvas.

5. Close the browser window.

6. Keep the project open for the next activity.

Student Activity: Customize Breakpoints

1. Ensure that the **ResponsiveScenarioMe** project is still open.

2. Change your magnification to **Best Fit** (View > Magnification).

3. Review the Breakpoints.

   ☐ select the **Desktop** Breakpoint (1024); notice that the bar turns purple

   ☐ select the **Tablet Portrait** Breakpoint (768); notice that the bar turns green

   ☐ select the **Mobile Portrait** Breakpoint (360); notice that the bar turns salmon

   You will learn the significance of the different color bars later.

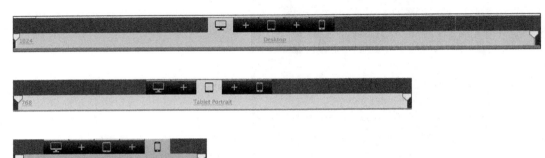

   As you alternate among the different Breakpoints, the objects on the canvas also change position. Note that only the objects within the colored horizontal bar will appear in the published lesson.

   Although the default Breakpoints are based on typical sizes of a desktop, tablet, and smart phone, you can easily adjust both the width and the height of any Breakpoint.

4. Manually adjust Breakpoints.

   ☐ if necessary, select the **Mobile Portrait** Breakpoint

   ☐ drag either Slider to decrease the width to **320** pixels (alternatively, you can highlight the number next to the left slider and type 320)

   Next you will adjust the Device Height. The ability to adjust a layout's height is disabled by default so that you don't accidentally change it. Each layout's default height provides space for Captivate's playbar. If you are not going to use a playbar in the published lesson, you should adjust the height accordingly.

5. Change the project Magnification to 75% (View > Magnification).

   If you are too close to the canvas, you will not be able to see the new height you are about to set. I've found that 75% is almost always the perfect magnification, but you may need to test several magnification levels to find the perfect magnification for your display.

6. Adjust the Device Height.

   ☐ ensure you are on the **Mobile Portrait** Breakpoint and then, on the **Properties Inspector**, **Style** tab click **Device Height**

   ☐ from the bottom of the canvas, drag the **Height Adjuster** down to **460**

Caution: When dragging the Height Adjuster (shown circled at the left), be careful not to grab the object on the slide by mistake. If you are having trouble dragging just the Height Adjuster, consider locking the image on the slide prior to dragging the Height Adjuster. (You can lock items via the far left of the Timeline.) Alternatively, you can type values directly into the field to the right of Device Height.

7. Review the different Breakpoints.

   ☐ select the **Tablet Portrait** Breakpoint

   ☐ select the **Desktop** Breakpoint

   Even though you changed the height on the Mobile Portrait Breakpoint, the height on the other two Breakpoints did not change.

   Next you will adjust the **Slide Height** independent of the **Device Height**. This technique is important if you need more real estate on your slide but do not want to change the Device Height.

   Note: Changing the Slide Height adds a scroll bar to the published lesson if the viewing device is not the same aspect ratio as the slide.

8. Change Slide Height.

   ❏ select the **Mobile Portrait** Breakpoint

   ❏ on the **Properties Inspector**, **Style** tab, notice there is a link symbol to the right of **Device Height**

   ❏ click the link symbol to **Unlink from the Device height**

   ❏ change the **Slide Height** (careful, **not** the Device Height) to **660**

Notice that the Device Height at the top of the canvas does not change; you've just added more real estate on your slide to add more objects. As mentioned earlier, when you publish the project, Captivate adds a scroll bar to the lesson so learners can scroll to see any content you added below the device height.

9. Link the Slide Height back to the Device Height.

   ❏ on the Properties Inspector, **Style** tab, click the link symbol to **Link to Device Height**

The Slide Height once again matches the Device Height (460 px).

Note: When you are determining your Breakpoints, it is helpful to know the viewport sizes (device size) of your audience. If you want to see a particular device size, visit viewportsizes.com. If you want to see the resolution of the device you are using, visit **http://viewportsizes.com/mine/**.

Breakpoints Confidence Check

1. Ensure that the **ResponsiveScenarioMe** project is still open.

2. Adjust the **Desktop** Breakpoint width to **1280**.

3. Adjust the **Desktop** Device Height to **720**.

4. Adjust the **Tablet Portrait** Breakpoint width to **1024**.

5. Adjust the **Tablet Portrait** Device Height to **768**.

6. Close the project (there is no need to save it).

Creating Responsive Projects

The process of creating a Responsive Project is nearly identical to creating a standard project. In a standard project, each of the slides must be the same size so you are prompted to specify an overall project size when creating a new, blank project. When you create a Responsive Project you aren't asked to decide on a project size. Instead, you'll control the size of each Breakpoint (layout) on a case-by-case basis.

Student Activity: Customize Theme Colors

1. Create a new Responsive Project.

   ❑ choose **File > New Project > Responsive Project**

2. Apply a Theme.

   ❑ on the Toolbar, click **Themes** and choose **Suave**

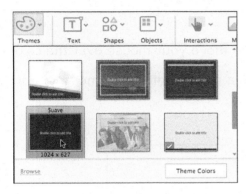

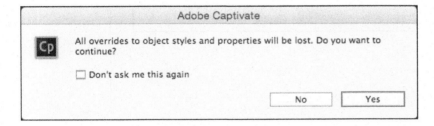

   ❑ click the **Yes** button

3. Preview the other two layouts.

   ❑ select the **Tablet Portrait** layout

   ❑ select the **Mobile Portrait** layout

   Themes in a Responsive Project contain objects that are responsive by default. When you select different Breakpoints, the canvas objects adjust to each layout automatically.

   ❑ return to the **Desktop** layout

   The Themes that come with Captivate are perfectly fine; however, you may have organizational standards for colors and font styles. You can easily adjust and save the Themes with your agency colors.

4. Customize the Theme colors.

❒ on the Toolbar, click **Themes** and then click the **Theme Colors** button

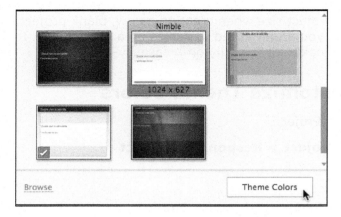

The Theme Colors dialog box opens.

❒ click the drop-down menu and then move your mouse over the colors

As you move over the colors, you see a preview of the theme colors on the canvas.

❒ select the **Clean** color theme

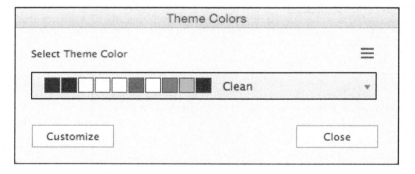

5. Customize the color palette.

❒ on the Theme Colors dialog box, click the **Customize** button

❒ click the word **Clean**

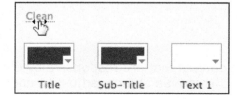

❏ change the name of the Theme Color to **my_theme**

❏ click any of the theme color boxes and change it to a desired color

Note: As you change the Theme colors, you won't see the changes on the canvas until after you click the Save button.

❏ click the **Save** button

Notice that your new color theme is displayed on the canvas and in the **Select Theme Colors** drop-down menu.

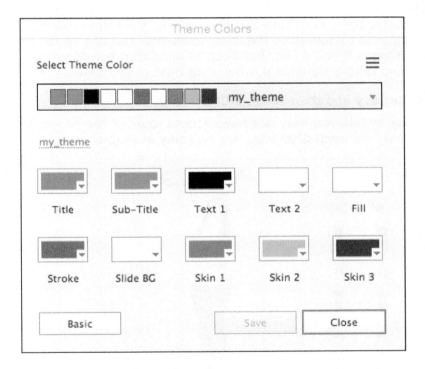

6. Close the Theme Colors dialog box.

7. Save the project to the Captivate9BeyondData folder as **my_responsivetheme**.

Editing a Responsive Project

Adding objects to a Responsive Project isn't any different than adding objects to a standard project. However, since Responsive Projects consist of three Breakpoints, the position of canvas objects may need to be adjusted for each layout. You'll use the Position Inspector to control an object's canvas position.

Student Activity: Use the Position Inspector

1. Ensure that the **my_responsivetheme** project is still open.

2. Select the Desktop layout.

3. Insert a Character.

   ❏ choose **Media > Characters**

   Note: If you have not yet downloaded the full set of Characters from the Adobe website, you likely have only a few Characters in each category. If you try to insert a Character you haven't yet downloaded, you will be prompted to download the missing assets. You can certainly download the images if you'd like, but keep in mind that the download is large and could take a significant amount of time to complete.

   ❏ select a **Category** and then select a **Character**

   ❏ select a **pose** (while you may not have access to all of the poses, the first couple of poses for each Character are typically available)

   ❏ click the **OK** button

   The character is inserted in the middle of the canvas.

   ❏ drag the character to the bottom **left** of the canvas

4. Review the character's position on the other Breakpoints.

    ❏ select the **Tablet Portrait** Breakpoint and then select the **Mobile Portrait** Breakpoint

    On the Mobile Portrait layout, the Character is not only smaller, but is positioned at the top of the canvas instead of the bottom. Initially, this automatic adjustment of objects seems fine. However, if you'd like an object (like the character) to remain fixed in a specific location, you need to adjust its Position Properties.

5. Select the **Desktop** Breakpoint and change the view Magnification to Best Fit so you can see the entire canvas. (**View > Magnification**)

6. Adjust the character's canvas position.

    ❏ on the canvas, double-click the character to open the **Properties Inspector**

    In a standard project, the Properties Inspector typically contains one or two inspectors: Properties and Timing. A responsive project introduces a third inspector: the **Position Inspector**.

    ❏ on the **Position Inspector**, click the **Bottom** drop-down menu and choose **%**

    ❏ replace the existing **Bottom** value with **2** and press [**enter**]

    ❏ click the **Right** drop-down menu and choose **%**

    ❏ replace the existing value with **0** and press [**enter**]

The character moves 2% from the bottom of the canvas and 0% from the right side of the canvas.

7. Review each of the project's Breakpoints.

   Although the image now stays at the bottom right of each canvas, the image still gets smaller as you move from Breakpoint to Breakpoint. Notice on the Position Inspector, Object Size area, that the default Object Size **Height** is set to Auto and **Width** is set to percent. To keep the Character the same size in all three layouts, you need to make another adjustment.

8. Adjust an object's Height and Width.

   ☐ select the **Desktop** Breakpoint

   ☐ select the character

   ☐ on the **Position Inspector**, **Object Size** area, change the Height to **%**

   ☐ change Width to **Auto**

   By setting an object's Height or Width to **Auto**, the object maintains its proportions from layout to layout.

9. Review each of the project's Breakpoints.

10. Adjust an object's position using pixels.

    ☐ select the **Desktop** layout

    ☐ select the character

    ☐ on the **Position Inspector**, **Object Size** area, change the Height to **px** (pixels)

    ☐ keep the Width set to **Auto**

11. Review each of the project's Breakpoints.

    By using **pixels** for the Height instead of a percentage, the image maintains its original size from layout to layout. However, notice on the Mobile Portrait layout that the image is now so big that it doesn't work with the layout. You'll adjust the position of the character on just the Mobile Portrait layout next.

Student Activity: Modify a Single Breakpoint

1. Ensure that the **my_responsivetheme** project is still open.

2. Adjust an object on a single layout.

   ☐ select the **Mobile Portrait** layout

   ☐ select the Character

   ☐ drag the character **down and to the right** so that only the top half of the image remains on the canvas

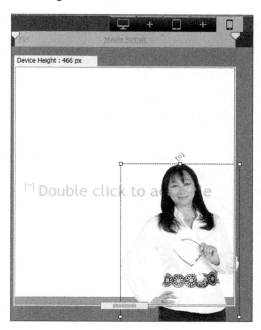

3. Review each of the project's other views (Breakpoints).

   Notice that the change you made to the character on the Mobile Portrait canvas has not affected the character on the other Breakpoints.

4. Select the **Mobile Portrait** view.

   With the character still selected, notice on the Position Inspector that the Object Position properties are **salmon**, while the Object Size properties are **purple**. The salmon color indicates properties that are unique to Mobile Portrait; purple indicates properties that are coming from the Desktop Breakpoint.

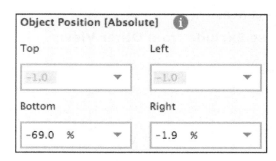

Student Activity: Exclude from View

1. Ensure that the **my_responsivetheme** project is still open.

2. Move an object to the Pasteboard.

   ❑ on the **Mobile Portrait** view, drag the character to the Pasteboard (the area outside the canvas)

   The character will not preview or publish when it is positioned on the Pasteboard. Let's see what's happened to the character on the other views.

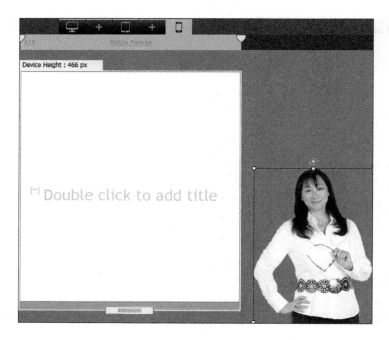

3. Review each of the project's views.

   Even though you positioned the character on the Pasteboard on the Mobile Portrait layout, the character still appears on both the Desktop and Tablet Portrait layouts. Manually dragging an object to the Pasteboard as a way of excluding it from a layout works great. But what if you want to exclude an object from multiple layouts... at one time?

4. Exclude an object from multiple views.

   ❑ select the **Tablet Portrait** Breakpoint

   ❑ choose **Shapes > Star**

   ❑ draw the star anywhere on the canvas

   ❑ right click on the star and choose **Exclude from Other Views**

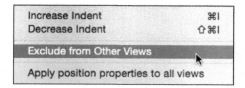

5. Review each of the project's Breakpoints.

   The star is automatically positioned on the Pasteboard for both the Desktop and Mobile Portrait views.

   Breakpoints have a parent (Desktop) to child (Tablet Portrait) to grandchild (Mobile Portrait) relationship. When you edit an object on the Desktop layout, the change will be seen on all of the views. However, when you edit an object on the Tablet Portrait layout, the edit appears only on the Tablet Portrait and Mobile Portrait views (not the Desktop layout). When you edit an object on the Mobile Portrait layout, the edit appears only on the Mobile Portrait layout, not the other layouts.

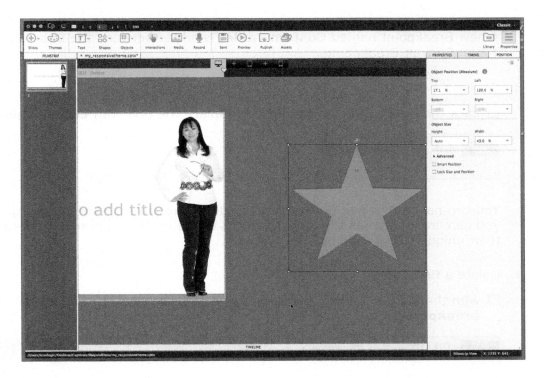

Student Activity: Add a New Breakpoint

1. Ensure that the **my_responsivetheme** project is still open.

2. Add a new Breakpoint.

    ❏ from between the Desktop and Tablet Portrait Breakpoints, click the **plus sign**

    A new Breakpoint named **Custom Tablet** is added between the Desktop and Tablet Portrait Breakpoints.

3. Rename a Breakpoint.

    ❏ click the words **Custom Tablet** and replace the text with **Larger Tablet**

    You can have up to five Breakpoints in Adobe Captivate. Using this feature, you can create layouts to meet the needs of the most common devices (and their unique sizes) used by your learners.

4. Delete a Breakpoint.

    ❏ with the **Larger Tablet** Breakpoint selected, click **Delete selected breakpoints**

    ❏ click the **Yes** button

5. Save and close the project.

Positioning Objects

When working with Responsive Projects, canvas objects can move and resize dramatically depending upon the Breakpoint being viewed. Captivate allows you to anchor objects to the canvas or to other objects.

Student Activity: Position and Link Objects

1. Open **MinMaxMe.cptx** from your Captivate9BeyondData folder.

2. Open the Master Slide panel (**Window > Master Slide**).

3. Insert an object on the Main Master slide.

    ❑ ensure the **Main Master** is selected (the Main Master slide is the largest of the masters and has the word **Nimble** just beneath it)

    ❑ ensure the **Desktop** Breakpoint is selected

    ❑ choose **Media > Image**

    ❑ open the **Captivate9BeyondData** folder

    ❑ from the **Cp8BeyondImages** folder, open **LogoCropped.bmp**

    The image is inserted in the middle of the Desktop view.

    ❑ on the **Position Inspector**, **Object Position [Absolute]** area, change the **Top** percent to **80**

    ❑ change the **Left** percent to **3**

    ❑ if necessary, change the **Object Size** Height to **Auto**

    ❑ change the **Object Size Width** percent to **8%**

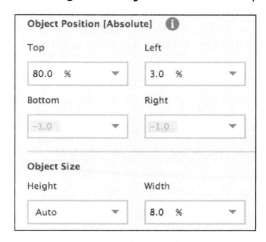

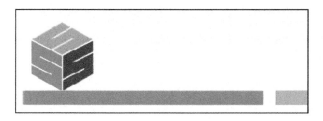

4. Review each of the project's Breakpoints.

   Notice that the image moves up a bit on each of the views. There will be instances where you're okay with an image moving higher on the view, but in this instance, you'd like it to stay in the same position, relative to the Breakpoint size.

5. Select the **Desktop** Breakpoint.

6. Zoom far enough away from the canvas so that you can see the entire canvas (and part of the surrounding Pasteboard).

7. Enable Smart Positioning.

   ❏ select the logo and, on the bottom of the Position Inspector, select **Smart Position** (if necessary)

   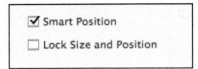

8. Anchor an object to the bottom of the canvas.

   ❏ ensure the logo is still selected

   ❏ at the top of the canvas, drag the top Smart Position marker (it's the gray object just above the 80%) down to the **bottom** of the canvas

   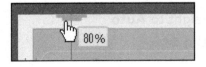

   ❏ when you see a horizontal line across the **entire bottom width of the canvas**, release your mouse

   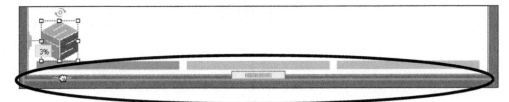

9. Review the Tablet Portrait and Mobile Portrait layouts.

   Notice that the position of logo is better—it does not float up as high on the canvas as before. However, the logo is still moving higher on the Tablet Portrait and Mobile Portrait layouts. Next you will anchor the logo to an another object on the canvas instead of the canvas.

10. Anchor an object to another object.

- ☐ select the **Desktop** layout
- ☐ if necessary, select the logo
- ☐ drag the Smart Position marker from the bottom of the canvas to the top of the red rectangle

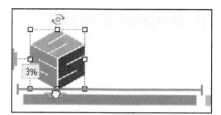

11. Review the Tablet Portrait and Mobile Portrait layouts.

   The logo now sticks to the relative position of the rectangle (instead of the canvas). But notice how small the logo gets, especially in the Mobile Portrait layout. Maybe your organization has standards for how big or small the logo can be. You'll set a maximum and minimum object size next.

12. Change the Min-Max Height and Width.

- ☐ select the **Desktop** layout
- ☐ select the logo and, on the **Position Inspector**, expand the **Advanced** area

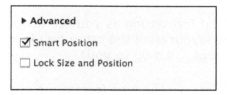

- ☐ change the **Min-Height** to **50** px and the **Min-Width** to **50** px

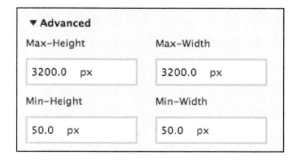

13. Review the Tablet Portrait and Mobile Portrait layouts.

   Notice that the size of the logo remains consistent from layout to layout. In fact, thanks to the Min-Height and Min-Width settings, the logo can never get smaller than 50 pixels.

14. Exit the Slide Master.

Responsive Styles

Do you have a need to use different fonts or font sizes for your text captions on each Breakpoint? Although you can manually change the font formatting on each caption, Breakpoint by Breakpoint, it would be much more efficient to use the Object Style Manager.

Student Activity: Edit Breakpoint Object Styles

1. Ensure that the **MinMaxMe** project is still open.

2. Edit the styles used by the Breakpoints.

   ☐ choose **Edit > Object Style Manager**

   ☐ from the list at the left, expand **Standard Objects**

   ☐ expand Smart Shapes

   ☐ select **Title**

   ☐ from the **Text Format** area at the right, notice that there are settings for each of the three project Breakpoints.

3. Select each Breakpoint and change the text formatting as you see fit (perhaps a smaller font size for the Mobile Portrait layout than the other two layouts or a different font for the Tablet Portrait layout... it's up to you).

4. When finished, click the **OK** button and observe the text formatting changes you've applied to each Breakpoint.

5. Save and close the project

Object Position Confidence Check

1. Open **ResponsivePositionMe** from the Captivate9BeyondData folder.

2. Click between the Tablet Portrait and the Mobile Portrait Breakpoints.

   As the male character changes position, the transparent text caption doesn't stay with him perfectly. You'll fix that next.

3. Select the **Desktop** Breakpoint and then select the caption.

4. On the **Position Inspector**, change the **Object Position (Absolute), Bottom** to **% Relative**.

5. Change the **Object Size, Height** to **% Relative**.

6. Select the male character.

7. On the Position Inspector, change the **Object Position, Bottom** to **% Relative**.

8. Change the **Object Size, Height** to **% Relative**.

9. Review the Tablet Portrait and Mobile Portrait layouts.

   Notice as the male character resizes and moves, the caption moves with him.

10. Save and close the project.

Notes

iCONLOGiC
"Skills and Drills" Learning

Module 11: Reporting Results

In This Module You Will Learn About:

And You Will Learn To:

LMS Reporting Options

Later in this module, you will publish a project and then upload it into a Learning Management System (LMS) called Inquisiq (you'll learn about Inquisiq on page 220). *But not so fast.* Before a project can be used with an LMS, you have to set up some reporting options and become familiar with the following: Sharable Content Object Reference Model (SCORM), Aviation Industry Computer-Based Training Committee (AICC), Sharable Content Object (SCO), and the Manifest File.

Sharable Content Object Reference Model

Developed by public- and private-sector organizations, SCORM is a series of eLearning standards that specifies ways to catalog, launch, and track course objects. Courses and management systems that follow the SCORM specifications allow for sharing of courses among federal agencies, colleges, and universities. Although SCORM is not the only eLearning standard (AICC is another), SCORM is one of the most common. There are two primary versions of SCORM—version 1.2, released in 1999, and version 2004.

During the remaining activities in this module, you will prepare and then publish a project to a SCORM-compliant LMS.

Aviation Industry Computer-Based Training Committee

AICC is an international association that develops guidelines for the aviation industry in the development, delivery, and evaluation of training technologies. When you publish your Captivate projects, you can specify SCORM or AICC compliance, but not both. Not sure which one to pick? Talk to your LMS provider for information on which one to use. When in doubt, consider that AICC is older and more established than SCORM, but SCORM is the standard most often used today.

Tin Can API

Today's learners are consuming eLearning content using a vast array of devices (PCs, Macs, and mobile devices, such as the iPad). And learners are working outside of traditional LMSs. In spite of these challenges, educators still need to capture reliable data about the learner experience.

The problem with data collection is that you need an expensive LMS to store the data. And your learners need live access to the LMS so that they can send the data. As mentioned above, the most widely used LMS standard for capturing data is SCORM. SCORM allows educators to track such things as learner completion of a course, pass/fail rates, and the amount of time a learner takes to complete a lesson or course. But what if a trainer needs to get scores from learners who are collaborating with other students using social media? What if the learners don't have access to the Internet?

The new Tin Can API allows training professionals to gather detailed data about the learner experience as the learner moves through an eLearning course (either online or offline). According to the Tin Can API website, "The Tin Can API (sometimes known as the **Experience API**) captures data in a consistent format about a person or group's activities from many technologies. Very different systems are able to securely communicate by capturing and sharing this stream of activities using Tin Can's simple vocabulary."

If the Tin Can API is supported by your LMS, you'll be happy to learn that it's also fully supported in Adobe Captivate. All you need to do is choose **Quiz > Quiz Preferences**. From the Reporting group, select **Enable reporting for this project**, select an LMS, and then select **TinCan** as the Standard.

Sharable Content Objects

Sharable Content Objects (SCOs) are standardized, reusable learning objects. An LMS can launch and communicate with SCOs and can interpret instructions that tell the LMS which SCO to show a user and when to show it. Why should you know what an SCO is? Actually, your Captivate projects are SCOs once you enable reporting (which you will learn to do on page 209). Next you will publish the project into a Content Package so that it can be uploaded into an LMS.

Student Activity: Set Quiz Reporting Options

1. Open **LMS_Me** from the Captivate9BeyondData folder.

2. Enable Reporting for the project.

   ☐ choose **Quiz > Quiz Preferences**

   The Preferences dialog box opens; Reporting is selected from the Quiz category.

   ☐ from the top of the dialog box, select **Enable reporting for this project**
   ☐ from the **LMS** drop-down menu, select **Other Standard LMSs**
   ☐ from the **Standard** drop-down menu, choose **SCORM 1.2**

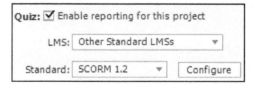

   SCORM 1.2, although an older standard, is still used by many LMS vendors today. Inquisiq (the LMS you will use shortly) supports SCORM 1.2, SCORM 2004, and AICC.

3. Set the Status Representation options.

   ☐ from the **Status Representation** area, select **Incomplete --->Complete**

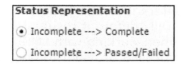

   This project isn't a conventional quiz—there are no question slides. Nevertheless, you can set interactive objects (such as buttons or click boxes) to report a value/score to the LMS, much like you can by assigning a point value to a question slide.

4. Set the Success/Completion Criteria.

❏ from the **Success/Completion Criteria** area, select **Slide views and/or quiz**

❏ deselect **Slide Views**

❏ select **Quiz** and ensure **Quiz is Passed** is selected from the drop-down menu

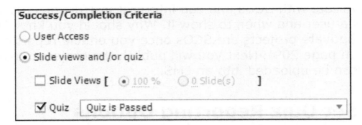

5. Set the Data to report.

❏ from the **Data To Report** area, select **Percentage**

Again, this project isn't a quiz at all. However, one of the objects in the lesson (a button) is going to be assigned a point value, making it a scoreable object. In essence, the lesson behaves much like a quiz. When the learner finishes with the lesson, the LMS displays the lesson as 100% Complete.

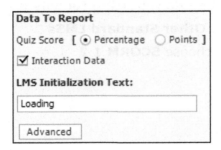

Note: The LMS Initialization Text field shown is not supported by every LMS. Fortunately, the LMS shown in this book supports the feature. Anything you type in the field appears just before the lesson begins to play for the learner. In essence, LMS Initialization Text serves as a second lesson Preloader. You can edit the text, if you'd like, or leave it set to the default (Loading).

Not every LMS fully supports the features in this dialog box (or the Manifest settings that you will set up next). And even if every feature is supported, each LMS could treat the features differently. One option might work perfectly in LMS A, while yielding totally different results in LMS B. The only consistent thing I have found when working with LMSs is that they can be inconsistent. Consult with your LMS provider to get an idea of what will work and what won't.

Manifest Files

The Manifest file allows your published Captivate projects to be used and launched from a SCORM 1.2- or 2004-compliant LMS. When you publish projects, you can have Captivate create the Manifest file for you. The Manifest file that Captivate creates contains XML tags that describe the organization and structure of the published project to the LMS.

Student Activity: Create a Manifest File

1. Ensure that the **LMS_Me** project is still open (the Quiz Preferences dialog box should also still be open via **Quiz > Quiz Preferences**).

2. Show the Manifest file options.

   ❏ from the top of the dialog box, ensure **SCORM 1.2** is selected (from the **Standard** drop-down menu)

   ❏ click the **Configure** button

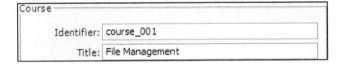

   The Manifest dialog box opens.

3. Set up the course information.

   ❏ in the **Identifier** field, type **course_001**

   The Identifier specifies a name used by the LMS to identify different manifests.

   ❏ in the **Title** field, type **File Management**

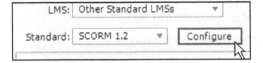

   The Title is seen by learners as they access the course on the LMS.
   A Description is not required. Depending on the LMS you use, the text may or may not appear in the LMS. If the feature is not supported by the LMS, it will likely be ignored, just like the Title. You'll leave the Description blank for this lesson.

   The Version number, which you left selected, can be used to distinguish manifests with the same identifier.

   There are two other optional choices in the Course area: Duration and Keywords. Duration lets you show how long it takes to complete the Captivate project. Keywords allows you to specify a short description. When the course is displayed via a browser, such as Internet Explorer, the description and Keywords can be searched like any web page.

211

4. Set up the SCO information.

☐ in the **SCO Identifier** field, type **sco_001**

The Identifier, which cannot contain spaces, specifies a name used by the LMS to identify different SCOs.

☐ in the **Title** field, type **Creating New Folders**

The Title you just typed shows up in the LMS. Although you can use spaces in the Title name, you should consider using short descriptive phrases.

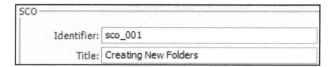

If you would like information on the remaining options in this dialog box, click the **Help** link at the bottom left of the dialog box.

☐ click the **OK** button to close the Manifest dialog box

☐ click the **OK** button to close the Preferences dialog box

Nothing about your project changes physically. However, once the project is published, it will automatically be zipped and capable of communicating with any SCORM-compliant LMS.

5. Save your work.

Advanced Interaction

If you are uploading content into an LMS, you will find the Advanced Interaction dialog box one of Captivate's most useful features. Using this handy screen, you can quickly determine what any of the interactive elements (click boxes, question slides, buttons, text entry boxes, etc.) are doing for the whole project—in one central location. You can determine, with a quick glance, which elements in your project are scoring, the number of allowed user-interaction attempts, the value of each interaction, and if the interaction should be tracked by the LMS. Prior to the Advanced Interaction feature, Captivate developers had to suffer through the laborious process of opening each slide and reviewing the interactive settings, object by object. If the developer missed just one object, the score sent to the LMS would likely be incorrect—a problem not discovered until after the lesson was published, uploaded to the LMS, and tested.

Student Activity: Report a Button Interaction

1. Ensure that the **LMS_Me** project is still open.

2. Enable Reporting for an object.

   ☐ go to slide **10**

   ☐ on the slide, double-click the large **Get Credit** button

   ☐ on the **Properties Inspector**, select the **Actions** tab

   ☐ from the **Reporting** area, select **Include in Quiz**

   ☐ change the Points to **100**

   ☐ select **Add to Total**

   ☐ select **Report Answers**

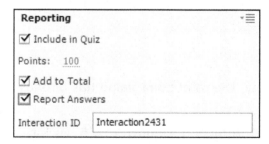

   There is an Interaction ID area containing an ID. Although some management systems require an Interaction ID for every object reporting a score, others do not. When in doubt, leave the Interaction ID set to the default value.

3. Save your work.

Student Activity: Adjust Slide Object Interaction

1. Ensure that the **LMS_Me** project is still open.

2. Display the Advanced Interaction window.

   ☐ choose **Project > Advanced Interaction**

   The Advanced Interaction window opens. Notice that the total score (as shown at the top of the dialog box) indicates that the lesson will report more than a perfect score to the LMS (112 points instead of 100). If you leave things the way they are, your LMS will likely report the results of the lesson incorrectly. Ideally, your lessons will never be worth more than 100 points.

   > Total: 112 Points

3. Disable reporting for two slide objects.

   ☐ from the **Slide/Object** column, row **3**, click the words **Click Box**

   Captivate jumps to slide 3 and automatically selects the Click Box on the slide.

   ☐ from the **Reporting** area of the **Properties Inspector**, notice that the Click Box is being included in the Quiz and is reporting a score of 11 points.

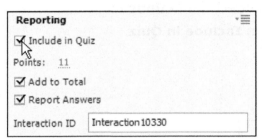

   ☐ deselect **Include in Quiz**

   On the Advanced Interaction window, the total point value has already dropped from 112 to 101.

   ☐ still working within the Advance Interaction window, row **6**, click the words **Click Box**

   ☐ from the **Reporting** area of the Properties Inspector, deselect **Include in Quiz**

   Notice that the total score for your lesson is now set to 100 points.

   > Total: 100 Points

4. Close the Advanced Interaction window and then save your work.

SCORM Preview

You will soon publish your Captivate project as a SCORM-compliant package so that it can report scores and interactions to an LMS. However, there could be something in your project that isn't reporting correctly. You won't know there's a problem until after you publish the project, upload it to your LMS, and then test it. To save you a significant amount of work, Captivate allows you to verify that your lesson will report accurately with an LMS via a feature called Preview in SCORM Cloud. An LMS preview window appears allowing you to debug your project in preview mode and view SCORM communication logs.

Student Activity: Preview in SCORM Cloud

1. Ensure that the **LMS_Me** project is still open.

2. Preview in SCORM Cloud.

   ☐ choose **Preview > Preview in SCORM Cloud**

   The SCORM Cloud dialog box opens.

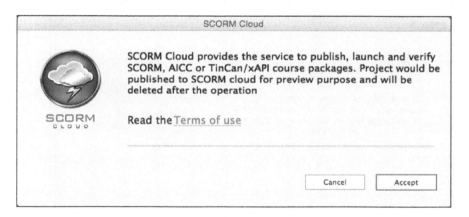

   ☐ click the **Accept** button

   The project will be uploaded to the SCORM Cloud.

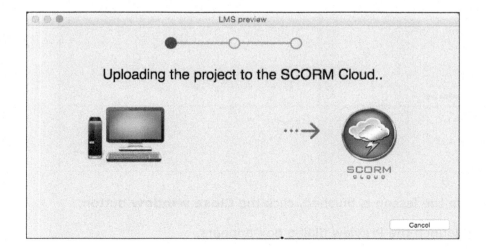

The lesson opens in a preview window. You can work through the lesson just as if it was published to an LMS.

❏ click through the lesson as prompted onscreen

As you work through the lesson, errors will be reported in the Communication logs area at the bottom of the preview. (There shouldn't be any errors because your lesson is, of course, absolutely perfect!)

❏ when you get to the credit screen, click the **Get Credit** button

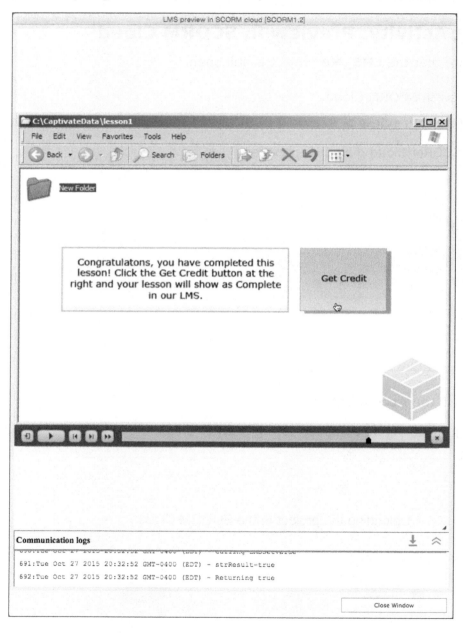

❏ when the lesson is finished, click the **Close window** button

The Relaunch the Preview dialog box appears.

☐ click the **Get Results** button

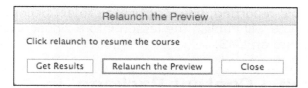

The Results window opens. At the bottom of the window, you can see that your lesson was worth 100 points and it scored correctly. Based on these results, you shouldn't have any errors after uploading the lesson to a SCORM-compliant LMS.

3. Close the Results window.

4. Close the Relaunch the Review dialog box.

Content Packages

As mentioned earlier, once you enable reporting, your Captivate project becomes a SCO. Now that the lesson is a SCO, you will Publish the lesson into a zipped Content Package so that it can be uploaded into an LMS.

Student Activity: Publish a Content Package

1. Ensure that the **LMS_Me** project is still open.

2. Review the Quiz Pass/Fail settings.

   ☐ choose **Quiz > Quiz Preferences**

   ☐ from the list of Categories at the left, select **Pass or Fail**

   From the **Pass/Fail Options** area, notice that the options have been set to 100% or more of total points to pass.

Pass/Fail Options: ⊙	100	% or more of total points to pass

   Because you enabled Reporting for the button on slide 10 and set it to 100 points, any learner who clicks the button will, thanks to the Pass/Fail options, pass the "Quiz."

   ☐ click the **Cancel** button

3. Publish a Content Package.

   ☐ choose **File > Publish**

   ☐ notice that **HTML5/SWF** is selected from the **Publish as** drop-down menu and that the **Project Title** is **CreateNewFolder**

4. Specify a Publish destination for the published package.

   ☐ click the **Browse** button (the yellow folder) and choose the **Captivate9BeyondData** folder

   Notice that Zip Files is selected. The Zip Files option is what creates the Content Package as you publish the lesson. Keep in mind that your published lesson is not just one file. In fact, there are several files that need to work together for the lesson to play and for the LMS to track and score it properly. Without the ability to create the Content Package, you would have to upload the published pieces into the LMS individually.

5. Specify an Output Format.

   ❐ from the **Output Format** Options area, select both **SWF** and **HTML5**

   Because you selected both SWF and HTML5, desktop users who have Flash will automatically be served the SWF version of the lesson when accessing the lesson. Learners who are using devices that do not support Flash will automatically be served the HTML5 version of the lesson.

   ❐ from the **Flash Player Version** drop-down menu, choose **Flash Player 10**

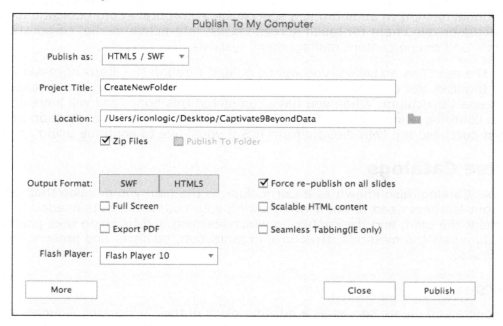

   ❐ click the **Publish** button

   ❐ click the **OK** button when the alert dialog box appears telling you the Publish process is complete

   When you look in the **Captivate9BeyondData** folder, you see a **CreateNewFolder.zip** file. This is the file you will soon import into the LMS. During the upload process, the Zip file is extracted, and the contents of the package are uploaded and then installed in the LMS.

6. Save and close the project.

Uploading to an LMS

An LMS handles issues related to providing access to the content, delivery of the content, and student performance tracking/reporting. In short, an LMS is the backbone of a web-based training system.

Inquisiq

Inquisiq is an easy-to-use LMS created by ICS Learning Group (ICS). ICS (**www.icslearninggroup.com**) is a leading provider of computer-based training solutions, including custom content development, LMS implementation, and instructional design. In addition, ICS specializes in corporate communications and multimedia development for touch-screen kiosks, interactive media, corporate websites, and online content management systems.

During the next few activities, you will be guided through the steps necessary to access Inquisiq, set up a user account, upload a content package, and create a Course and Curriculum. When you have completed this book, you will have up to 30 days to continue using Inquisiq free of charge. At the end of the evaluation period, you can purchase the LMS directly from ICS if you'd like to continue using its LMS.

Course Catalogs

A Course Catalog, also known as a Curriculum, is the plan you develop that details what your learners need to know when taking your courses, assets needed to implement the plan, and the context in which learning and teaching take place. The Curriculum sets the methods, structure, organization, balance, and presentation of the courses.

Courses

Each course you create serves as a building block of the Curriculum. Courses as they relate to learning are a series of lessons or steps that, when completed, fulfill the plan specified by the Curriculum. Each of the following could be considered a course: lectures, discussions, simulations, assignments, tests, and exams.

> **Note:** You will next set up a free account on Inquisiq and upload the SCO you published on page 218. You must have Internet access to complete the remaining activities in this module.

Student Activity: Create an Inquisiq LMS Account

1. Create a user account in Inquisiq.

   ❏ using a web browser go to **www.inquisiqr4.com**

   ❏ at the top of the page, click the **Free LMS Trial** button

   The Inquisiq R3 LMS Free Trial Account page opens.

2. Specify an Account Name and Password.

   ❏ fill in the **Account Name** field with your **first and last name** (the name you enter here will become part of the domain name used for your account... you can use **any name** except the one shown below, but don't use spaces)

* **Inquisiq LMS Account Name**	• Must be at least 3 characters and no more than 50 characters. • May only contain letters (not case-sensitive), numbers or dashes (-).

   sammiebifferson

   Your Free Trial Account URL will be:

   http://sammiebifferson.inquisiqr4.com

   ❏ notice that your Username will be **administrator** by default

   ❏ type **a password** into the **Password** field

   You need to remember the Domain Name and Password to log into the LMS during your 30-day trial period. The password must contain at least six characters and cannot be the word **password**.

* **Username**	administrator
* **Password**	• Must be at least 6 characters and no more than 25 characters. • Cannot contain 'password', '123456', '654321' or contain the username. •••••••• Confirm by entering again: ••••••••

   ❏ continue to fill in the required fields (Name, Company Name, and Email) and agree to the User Agreements

   Note: You might also want to deselect "YES; contact me for a personal live product tour and free consultation."

   ❏ click the **Create a Free Trial of Inquisiq R3 LMS** button

   Once the trial account has been set up, a confirmation screen opens.

   ❏ click the **URL** link to open the start page for the LMS trial

   Inquisiq LMS URL: http://sammiebifferson.inquisiqr4.com

3. Login to the LMS.

❐ at the far right of the screen, type your **Username** and **Password** into the two fields (your username is administrator)

Username:

administrator

Password (case-sensitive):

••••••••

Login

❐ click the **Login** button

By default, you are taken to the Inquisiq R3 Administrator Menu.

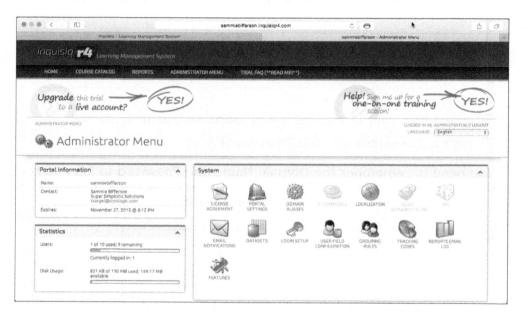

4. Upload a SCORM Package.

❐ from the Content area at the bottom of the page, click **SCORM Packages**

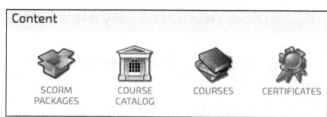

Content

SCORM PACKAGES   COURSE CATALOG   COURSES   CERTIFICATES

The SCORM Packages screen opens.

❏ from the Actions area at the far right of the window, click the **Upload SCORM Package** link

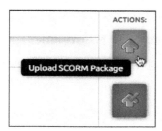

The Upload screen appears.

❏ click the **Choose File** button
❏ navigate to **Captivate9BeyondData** folder
❏ open the **CreateNewFolder.zip** file you created on page 218

❏ click the **Upload** button

The package is imported into the LMS.

❏ click the **Close** button

Student Activity: Create an LMS Course

1. Ensure that you are still logged into your Inquisiq account.

2. Create a new course.

   ☐ from the top of the window, click the **Administrator Menu** link

   ☐ from the Content area at the bottom of the page, click **Courses**

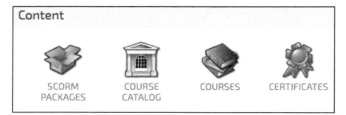

The Courses pages appears.

   ☐ at the upper right of the Courses screen, click **New Course**

   ☐ in the **Name** field, name the new course **File Management**

   ☐ in the **Short Description** field, type **These interactive lessons will teach you such fundamental Windows skills as creating folders, renaming folders, setting up a folder hierarchy, and Recycling.**

   ☐ from the bottom of the page, click the **Save Changes** button

The following screen appears.

Student Activity: Attach a Lesson to a Course

1. Ensure that you are still logged into your Inquisiq account.

2. Attach an SCO to a course.

   ❏ from the top of the window, click the **Administrator Menu** link

   ❏ from the Content area at the bottom of the page, click **Courses**

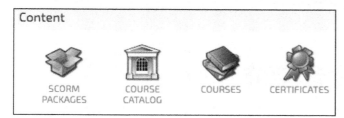

The File Management course is listed among the courses within the LMS.

   ❏ at the far right of the File Management row, click the **Modify** icon (the pencil)

The course opens for editing.

   ❏ from the **Tools** area at the right of the Courses page, click **Lessons**

The **Lessons** page for the File Management course opens.

   ❏ from the **Actions** area at the right side of the Lessons page, click **New Online Lesson**

The Add Lesson window appears.

   ❏ in the **Name** field, name the lesson **Creating New Folders**

*Name:	Creating New Folders
*Type:	Online Lesson ▾

❏ in the **Short Description** field, type **This lesson will teach you how to create a new folder on your computer.**

❏ from the **Package/Resource** area, click the **Select Package/Resource** button

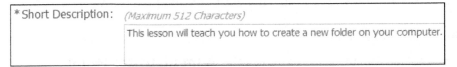

The Packages window opens. This is where you find any content packages that you have uploaded to the LMS. In this instance, you see your CreateNewFolder.zip package that you uploaded earlier, along with several assets that are included with the Inquisiq trial account.

❏ select the **CreateNewFolder.zip** package

❏ click the **OK** button

❏ from the list of resources, select **sco_001_RES**

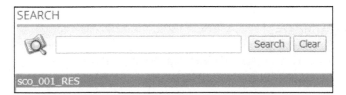

❏ click the **OK** button

❏ from the bottom of the page, click the **Save Changes** button

3. Publish a course.

☐ from the top of the window, click the **Administrator Menu** link

☐ from the bottom of the window, click **Courses**

☐ from the **Published** column, click the gray check mark for the File Management course

You will be asked to confirm the Publish action.

☐ click the **OK** button

Once the course is published, the gray check mark turns green. The final steps are to create a Catalog and attach the File Management course to the catalog so that it can be accessed by your online learners.

Student Activity: Create an LMS Catalog

1. Ensure that you are still logged into your Inquisiq account.

2. Add a Catalog (Curriculum) to the LMS.

   ❑ from the top of the window, click the **Administrator Menu** link

   ❑ from the bottom of the screen, click **Course Catalog**

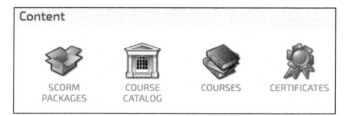

   ❑ from the **Actions** area at the right side of the window, click **New Catalog**

The Add Catalog window appears.

   ❑ in the **Name** area, type **Windows Training**

   ❑ in the **Short Description** area, type **Everything you ever wanted to know about Windows, but were afraid to ask.**

   ❑ from the bottom of the window, click the **Save Changes** button and close the window

The new catalog now appears in the Course Catalogs menu.

Student Activity: Attach a Course to a Catalog

1. Ensure that you are still logged into your Inquisiq account.

2. Attach a course to a catalog.

   ☐ select the **Windows Training** Catalog

   ☐ from the Actions area at the far right of the window, click **Add Course(s) To Catalog**

The Courses window opens. The File Management course you added is included within the list, along with other courses included in the Inquisiq trial account.

   ☐ select the **File Management** course

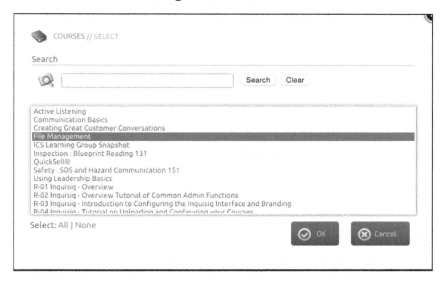

   ☐ click the **OK** button twice to close both dialog boxes

Student Activity: Test an eLearning Course

1. Logout of the LMS.

   ☐ at the upper right of the LMS window, click the **Logout** link

   Logged in as: ADMINISTRATOR / Logout

   You cannot test the lesson while logged in as an administrator. The Inquisiq trial account includes a "learner" account that allows you to test the course.

2. Login to the LMS using the learner account.

   ☐ at the upper right of the LMS window, type **learner** into the **Username** field

   ☐ in the **Password** field, type **inquisiq**

   ☐ click the **Login** button

   Because this is the first time you are using the "learner" account, you are required to create a new password.

   ☐ type any password you like (you can use the same password that you used when you created the administrator account but remember the password if you want to access the account later)

   ☐ after you have changed the password, click the **Change Password** button

   ☐ click the **Continue** button

3. Test the File Management course you added earlier.

   ☐ from the menu at the top of the window, click **Course Catalog**

   ☐ from the list of Catalogs, click **Windows Training**

    Catalog: Windows Training
   Everything you ever wanted to know about Windows, but were afraid to ask.

   The File Management course you created, published, and attached to the catalog is the only course available. In a real catalog, there would likely be multiple courses, each containing multiple lessons.

   ☐ click the **File Management** course title

   ☐ click the **Enroll** icon

File Management

‹ BACK TO PARENT CATALOG

Enroll   ☆☆☆☆☆
                Average of 0 ratings: Not rated yet

❏ from the top of the page, click **My Account**

The course is available in the list of available lessons.

❏ from the right side of the window, click the green **Go** icon

Notice that the status of the Creating New Folders lesson shows as **Not Attempted**.

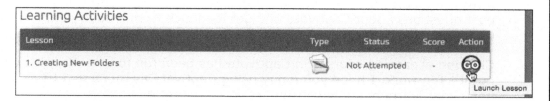

❏ from the right side of the window, click the green **Go** icon

4. Work through the lesson (click the **Continue** button on the first slide and then move through the lesson as instructed onscreen).

5. When you get to the end of the lesson, click the **Get Credit** button. (Remember, this button is worth 100 points and lets the LMS know that the learner has completed the lesson.)

6. When you reach the end of the lesson, close the lesson window. (After the window closes, the LMS saves the data.)

Data Saved.
Click here to go back to the course details page.

7. Click the word **here** to go back to the course details page.

And like magic, the status of the lesson has changed from **Not Attempted** to **Completed** and **100%**.

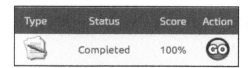

8. Logout of the LMS.

❏ click the **Logout** link in the upper right of the window

9. Close the web browser.

Congratulations, you have completed this book! If you've also worked through *Adobe Captivate 9: The Essentials*, you have just about all of the knowledge you need to create compelling eLearning lessons. If you want to become a Captivate master, practice will indeed make perfect. I encourage you to begin using Captivate right away... and use it frequently. There is truly no substitute for hands-on experience using the tool.

If you are looking for more information about Adobe Captivate, I encourage you to visit my blog (iconlogic.blogs.com). I typically post articles a few times each week about eLearning, Captivate, and technical communications. You might also want to visit the Captivate user community (http:// forums.adobe.com/community/adobe_captivate) where you will be able to post questions about Captivate and get feedback from industry experts. The Captivate blog (http://blogs.adobe.com/captivate/) is also a useful site.

Creating eLearning courses in Captivate has been fun for me. Yes, it's work... but it's fun work. I hope you enjoy using Captivate as much as I have. And I hope your learners enjoy consuming your content even more.

Index

CPSIA information can be obtained
at www.ICGtesting.com
Printed in the USA
LVOW02s0555020517

532923LV00016B/1087/P

9 781932 733907